ב"ה

TORAH STUDIES

Torah Studies

Season Three 5775

Student Manual

JEWISH LEARNING INSTITUTE

The ROHR JEWISH LEARNING INSTITUTE
*gratefully acknowledges
the pioneering support of*

George & Pamela
Rohr

Since its inception,
the JLI has been
a beneficiary of the vision,
generosity, care and concern
of the Rohr family.

*In the merit of
the tens of thousands of hours
of Torah study
by JLI students worldwide,
may they be blessed with health,
Yiddishe nachas from all their loved ones,
and extraordinary success
in all of their endeavors.*

Contents

SHEMINI

Something's Fishy

Always Consider the Source

Student Manual

PARSHA OVERVIEW
Shemini

On the eighth day, following the seven days of their inauguration, Aaron and his sons begin to officiate as kohanim (priests); a fire issues forth from G-d to consume the offerings on the altar, and the divine presence comes to dwell in the Sanctuary.

Aaron's two elder sons, Nadav and Avihu, offer a "strange fire before G-d, which He commanded them not" and die before G-d. Aaron is silent in face of his tragedy. Moses and Aaron subsequently disagree as to a point of law regarding the offerings, but Moses concedes to Aaron that Aaron is in the right.

G-d commands the kosher laws, identifying the animal species permissible and forbidden for consumption. Land animals may be eaten only if they have split hooves and also chew their cud; fish must have fins and scales; a list of non-kosher birds is given, and a list of kosher insects (four types of locusts).

Also in Shemini are some of the laws of ritual purity, including the purifying power of the mikvah (a pool of water meeting specified qualifications) and the wellspring. Thus the people of Israel are enjoined to "differentiate between the impure and the pure."

1. Fins and Scales

Kosher Fish

TEXT 1

Vayikra 11:9-10

אֶת זֶה תֹּאכְלוּ מִכֹּל אֲשֶׁר בַּמָּיִם כֹּל אֲשֶׁר לוֹ סְנַפִּיר וְקַשְׂקֶשֶׂת בַּמַּיִם בַּיַּמִּים וּבַנְּחָלִים אֹתָם תֹּאכֵלוּ:

וְכֹל אֲשֶׁר אֵין לוֹ סְנַפִּיר וְקַשְׂקֶשֶׂת בַּיַּמִּים וּבַנְּחָלִים מִכֹּל שֶׁרֶץ הַמַּיִם וּמִכֹּל נֶפֶשׁ הַחַיָּה אֲשֶׁר בַּמָּיִם שֶׁקֶץ הֵם לָכֶם:

Among all [creatures] that are in the water, you may eat these: Any [of the creatures] in the water that has fins and scales, those you may eat, whether [it lives] in the waters, in the seas, or in the rivers.

But any [creatures] that do not have fins and scales, whether in the seas or in the rivers, among all the creeping creatures in the water and among all living creatures that [live] in the water, are an abomination for you.

Bottom Dwellers

TEXT 2

Nachmanides, Pirush Haramban Vayikra ad loc.

וטעם הסנפיר והקשקשת, כי בעליהן שוכנים לעולם בעליון המים ובצלוליהן ויקבלו גידול באויר הנכנס שם, ולכן יש בהם קצת חום דוחה מהם שפעת הליחות כאשר יעשה הצמר והשער וגם הצפרנים באדם ובבהמה.

ושאין לו סנפיר וקשקשת ישכון לעולם בתחתיות המים ובעכוריהם ולרוב הלחות ואפיסת החום לא ידחה מהם דבר, ועל כן הם בעלי לחה קרה דבקה קרובה להמית, והיא ממיתה בקצת המימות כאגמים המעופשים.

Rabbi Moshe ben Nachman
(Nachmanides, Ramban)
1194–1270

Scholar, philosopher, author and physician. Nachmanides was born in Spain and served as leader of Iberian Jewry. In 1263, he was summoned by King James of Aragon to a public disputation with Pablo Cristiani, a Jewish apostate. Though Nachmanides was the clear victor of the debate, he had to flee Spain because of the resulting persecution. He moved to Israel and helped reestablish communal life in Jerusalem. He authored a classic commentary on the Pentateuch and a commentary on the Talmud.

The reason for the requirement of fins and scales is that creatures which possess these features dwell in the upper, clearer part of the waters, living in an environment with more oxygen. Thus, they possess some degree of warmth with which to counter the influence of moisture, as is the function of hair, fur, and nails in humans and animals.

Aquatic creatures that do not have fins and scales are bottom dwellers that live in murkier waters. Due to the excessive moisture and lack of warmth, they cannot repel anything. Thus, they carry cold moisture almost to the degree of causing death. Indeed, this does cause death in some waters such as rotten swamps.

TEXT 3

Sefer Hachinuch
A work on the biblical commandments. Four aspects of every mitzvah are discussed in this work: the definition of the mitzvah; ethical lessons that can be deduced from the mitzvah; basic laws pertaining to the observance of the mitzvah; and who is obligated to perform the mitzvah and when. The work was composed in the 13th century by an anonymous author who refers to himself as "the Levite of Barcelona." It has been widely thought that this referred to Rabbi Aharon Halevi of Barcelona (Re'ah); however, this view has been contested.

Rabbi Aharon of Barcelona, Sefer Hachinuch §154

יודע אלקים כי כל המאכלות שהרחיק מעמו אשר בחר יש בהם נזקים מצויים לגופים, אשר הם כלים לנפשות לפעול בהם ולהתעלות על ידי מעשיהם הטובים, ועל כן הרחיקנו מהם למען יפעלו הנפשות פעולתן ולא ינעלו בפניהם רוע מזג הגופות וטמטום הלבבות.

It is known before G-d that all the foods which He banned for His chosen nation are harmful to the body. The body is a vehicle for the soul to operate in and be elevated through the performance of good deeds. So, G-d commanded us to abstain from certain [harmful] foods to enable the soul to perform unhindered by an unhealthy imbalance within the body and the dulling of the heart.

Visible Scales

Babylonian Talmud
A literary work of monumental proportions that draws upon the legal, spiritual, intellectual, ethical, and historical traditions of Judaism. The 37 tractates of the Babylonian Talmud contain the teachings of the Jewish sages from the period after the destruction of the 2nd Temple through the 5th century CE. It has served as the primary vehicle for the transmission of the Oral Law and the education of Jews over the centuries; it is the entry point for all subsequent legal, ethical, and theological Jewish scholarship.

TEXT 4

Talmud Tractate Avodah Zara 39a

רב אשי איקלע לטמדוריא, אייתו לקמיה ההוא נונא דהוה דמי לצלופחא, נקטיה להדי יומא, חזא דהוה ביה צימחי ושרייה.

When Rabbi Ashi visited Tamduria, they set before him a fish resembling an eel; holding it up against the sun, he noticed that it had small scales, so he declared it permitted. +

TEXT 5

Rabbi Yechiel Michel Epstein, Aruch Hashulchan Yoreh Dei'ah 83:15

יש מיני דגים טהורים שקשקשיהם דקים מאד ואינם ניכרים ולכן אם
כרכוהו בבגד או נתנו אותו בכלי מלא מים ונמצאו קשקשים מותר דלא
הצריכה התורה קשקשים גדולים דווקא ולכן במינים שאינם ידועים לנו
ועשו בחינה בכריכת בגד או במים ונמצאו קשקשים היא כשרה וכן אם
העמידו הדג נגד השמש ורואין בו קשקשים קטנים מותר...
ודע שדבר פשוט הוא דבדבר שצריך ראיית עין אינו מועיל אם רואין על
ידי זכוכית המגדלת הראיה וצריך לראות בעין עצמה וכן הוא בעניינים
שבכל התורה כולה במה שצריך ראיית עין.

Rabbi Yechiel Michel Halevi Epstein
1829–1908
Noted author of Jewish law. Rabbi Epstein lived in Czarist Lithuania and was chief rabbi of Novozypkov, a town near Minsk, and later, of Navahrudak, where he served until his death. A prolific writer, his primary work is *Aruch Hashulchan*, an expanded and reworked code of Jewish law.

There are certain kosher fish with very small scales that are difficult to identify and can only be discerned in water or by tying a cloth around them. These fish are nevertheless kosher, for the Torah does not require that the scales be large. Accordingly, if a previously unknown species of fish is tested as described above and scales are found, it is kosher. Similarly, if it is scrutinized by the sunlight and tiny scales are found, it is kosher…

It is clear that for matters which require visible discernment, seeing through a magnifying glass does not count, rather it must be visible to the naked eye. This rule applies to all halachic matters that require human vision.

Falling Off

TEXT 6

Rabbi Yosef Caro
(Maran, *Beit Yosef*)
1488–1575
Halachic authority and author.
Rabbi Caro was born in Spain,
but was forced to flee during
the expulsion in 1492 and
eventually settled in Safed,
Israel. He authored many
works including the *Beit Yosef*,
Kesef Mishneh, and a mystical
work, *Magid Meisharim*.
Rabbi Caro's magnum opus,
the Shulchan Aruch (Code
of Jewish Law), has been
universally accepted as the
basis for modern Jewish law.

Shulchan Aruch Yoreh Dei'ah 83:1

סימני דגים מפורשים בתורה: כל שיש לו סנפיר וקשקשת, טהור. וסנפיר, הוא ששט בו. וקשקשת, הן הקליפות הקבועות בו... ואפילו אין לו עתה, ועתיד לגדלם לאחר זמן או שהיה לו בעודו במים והשירן מיד בעלותו ליבשה, מותר.

The indicia for fish are stated clearly in the Torah—"snapir" and "kaskeset." "Snapir" are the fins used to swim, and "kaskeset" are the scales attached to the body… If a fish does not currently have scales but would have grown them in the future, or it had scales that were shed as it was brought ashore, it is kosher.

One without the Other

TEXT 7A

Talmud Tractate Nidah 51b

כל שיש לו קשקשת, יש לו סנפיר, ויש שיש לו סנפיר ואין לו קשקשת.

All fish that have scales have fins, but there are some that have fins and no scales.

TEXT 7B

Shulchan Aruch Ibid. 83:3

כל שיש לו קשקשת יש לו סנפיר, ויש שיש לו סנפיר ואין לו קשקשת.
לפיכך מצא מצא חתיכת דג שיש לו קשקשת, אין צריך לחזור אחר סנפיר.
מצא לו סנפיר, לא יאכלנו עד שידע שיש לו קשקשת.

ll fish that have scales have fins, but there are some that have fins and no scales. Thus, one who finds pieces of fish with scales need not look for fins, whereas one who finds a piece of fish with fins should not eat it unless he knows that it also has scales.

2. It's all about the Scales

Peelable

TEXT 8

Nachamanides, Ibid.

"קשקשת, אלו הקבועים בו". לשון רש"י. וכן הוא בגמרא במסכת
חולין. אבל לא תבין מלשונם שהן קבועים בגופן ממש ודבוקים בעור
הדג, אבל קראום "קבועים" שאינן נדין ממנו ולא מזדעזעין בו כסנפיה.
והם הקליפין העגולים שגלדן דומה לצפורן, שהם נפשטין מעור הדג
ביד או בסכין, אבל כל שהוא קבוע ודבוק בעור הדג ואינו נפרד מן העור
כלל אינו קשקשת, ובעליו אסור הוא.

Rashi writes "Kaskeset *are affixed to the body of the fish." The same term appears in the Talmud in Tractate Chulin. However, do not make the mistake of assuming that it means that the scales must be entirely part of the body; the meaning of the word "affixed" in this context is that it does not move and flap around as do the fins. The reference is to the round, fingernail-like scales that can be filleted off the fish's body with one's hand or a knife. However, anything permanently attached to the dermis of the fish and cannot be removed are not considered "scales," and such fish are not kosher.*

TEXT 9

Rabbi Yechezkel Landau, Responsa Noda Beyehuda,
Second Edition, Yoreh Dei'ah §28

וגוף החומרא שהמציא רבינו הרמב"ן בפירוש התורה בפרשת שמיני
שאם אינם נקלפים כלל לא נחוש בו לסימן טהרה אלמלא אמרה אדם
אחר הייתי דן כנגדו...

אבל מה אעשה ורבינו הגדול הרמב"ן אמרה והרב המגיד משנה בפרק
א' ממאכלות אסורות הביאו, והרב בית יוסף בריש סימן פ"ג הביאו
ורמ"א קבעו בהג"ה, צריכין אנו לכוף אזנינו ולשמוע דבריהם באימה.

I n his commentary to the Torah, Nachmanides developed the following requirement: that the scales must be able to be peeled off the fish's body, and if not, they do not qualify as indicia of kashrut. If another man would have said it, I would refute it…

But what can I do—Nachmanides the great has uttered it! Further, the Maggid Mishneh cites it, the Bet Yosef cites it too, and the Rema establishes it as the accepted ruling. So, we must bend our ears and hearken to their words with reverence.

Rabbi Yechezkel Landau
(*Noda BiYehudah*)
1713–1793

Halachist. Rabbi Landau was born in Poland. In 1755, he assumed the rabbinate of Prague and all of Bohemia. An influential authority on Halachah, he responded to queries from all over Europe, most of which have been collected and published in *Responsa Noda BiYehudah.* He also wrote explanatory commentaries on the Shulchan Aruch and a commentary on several Talmudic tractates.

Question—Why Mention it?

TEXT 10

Talmud Tractate Nidah 51b

מכדי, אנן אקשקשת סמכינן, סנפיר דכתב רחמנא למה לי?... ולכתוב
רחמנא קשקשת ולא בעי סנפיר!
אמר רבי אבהו, וכן תנא דבי רבי ישמעאל "יגדיל תורה ויאדיר".

Now consider: Because we rely on scales [alone], what need then was there for the All Merciful to mention fins?... Why did not the All Merciful write "scales" and there would be no need for the mention of fins?

Rabbi Avahu said and so it was also taught in the school of Rabbi Yishmael: To make the Torah great and glorious.

3. Kosher Learning

Immersed in Torah

TEXT 11

Talmud Tractate Ta'anit 7a

אמר רבי חנינא בר אידי: למה נמשלו דברי תורה למים, דכתיב "הוי כל
צמא לכו למים"?

לומר לך: מה מים מניחין מקום גבוה והולכין למקום נמוך, אף דברי
תורה אין מתקיימין אלא במי שדעתו שפלה.

Rabbi Chanina bar Ida said: Why are the words of the Torah likened unto water, as it is written [in reference to the Torah], "Ho, all who are thirsty, come for water?"

This is to teach you, just as water flows from a higher level to a lower level, so, too, the words of the Torah endure only with one who is humble.

TEXT 12

Talmud Tractate Berachot 61b

פעם אחת גזרה מלכות הרשעה שלא יעסקו ישראל בתורה, בא פפוס בן יהודה ומצאו לרבי עקיבא שהיה מקהיל קהלות ברבים ועוסק בתורה. אמר ליה "עקיבא, אי אתה מתירא מפני מלכות"?

אמר לו: אמשול לך משל, למה הדבר דומה—לשועל שהיה מהלך על גב הנהר, וראה דגים שהיו מתקבצים ממקום למקום, אמר להם "מפני מה אתם בורחים"? אמרו לו "מפני רשתות שמביאין עלינו בני אדם". אמר להם "רצונכם שתעלו ליבשה, ונדור אני ואתם כשם שדרו אבותי עם אבותיכם"? אמרו לו "אתה הוא שאומרים עליך פקח שבחיות? לא פקח אתה, אלא טפש אתה! ומה במקום חיותנו אנו מתיראין, במקום מיתתנו על אחת כמה וכמה"!

אף אנחנו, עכשיו שאנו יושבים ועוסקים בתורה, שכתוב בה כי הוא חייך וארך ימיך, כך, אם אנו הולכים ומבטלים ממנה, על אחת כמה וכמה!

O nce, the wicked government [the Roman Empire] decreed that the Jewish people were forbidden to study Torah. Papus ben Judah saw Rabbi Akiva convening gatherings in public and studying Torah with them. Said he to him, "Akiva, are you not afraid of the government?"

Said Rabbi Akiva to him, "I'll give you a parable."

"A fox was walking along a river and saw fish rushing to and fro. Said the fox to the fish, 'Why are you fleeing?'

"Said they to him, 'We are fleeing the nets that the humans spread for us.'

"Said he to them, 'Why don't you come out onto the dry land? We'll live together!'

"Said they to him, 'Are you the one of whom it is said is the wisest of animals? You're not wise, but foolish! If, in our environment of life, we have cause for fear, how much more so in the environment of our death!'

"The same applies to us [said Rabbi Akiva]: If, now, when we sit and study the Torah, of which it is said, 'For it is your life and the lengthening of your days,' such is our situation, how much more so if we abandon it!"

Yirat Shamayim

TEXT 13

Talmud Tractate Shabbat 31a

אמר רבא: בשעה שמכניסין אדם לדין אומרים לו "נשאת ונתת באמונה? קבעת עתים לתורה? עסקת בפריה ורביה? צפית לישועה? פלפלת בחכמה? הבנת דבר מתוך דבר?"

ואפילו הכי, אי יראת ה' היא אוצרו, אין; אי לא, לא.

משל לאדם שאמר לשלוחו "העלה לי כור חיטין לעלייה". הלך והעלה לו. אמר לו "עירבת לי בהן קב חומטון"? אמר לו "לאו". אמר לו "מוטב אם לא העליתה".

Rava said: When man is brought in for Judgment he is asked, "Did you deal with integrity? Did you fix times for Torah study? Did you engage in procreation? Did you anticipate the redemption? Did you engage in the dialectics of wisdom? Did you understand one thing from another?

Yet, even so [even if he did study Torah, and to the full extent described], if "the fear of G-d is his treasure [i.e., he lived with fear of G-d]," we accept it; if not, it is not accepted.

This is comparable to one who instructed his agent, "Bring up for me a kor of wheat to the loft," and he went and did so. "Did you mix in a kab of chumton?" he asked him. "No," replied he. "Then it were better that you had not carried it up at all!" he retorted.

Growing in Learning

TEXT 14

Rabbi Shneur Zalman of Liadi, Torah Ohr 38c; 39d

לימוד התורה צריך דוקא ללמוד בכל יום דבר חדש...

תורה היא צריכה דוקא התחדשות.

עיין זוהר בראשית בהקדמה "ולאפשא לה בכל יומא".

Proper Torah study requires that one learn something new every day...

Torah requires novelty. See Zohar, introduction to Bereishit, "To discover new insight every day."

Rabbi Shneur Zalman of Liadi (Alter Rebbe) 1745–1812

Chasidic rebbe, halachic authority, and founder of the Chabad movement. The Alter Rebbe was born in Liozna, Belarus, and was among the principal students of the Magid of Mezeritch. His numerous works include the *Tanya*, an early classic containing the fundamentals of Chabad Chasidism, and *Shulchan Aruch HaRav*, a code of Jewish law.

Fins without Scales, Scales with Fins

TEXT 15A

The Lubavitcher Rebbe, Reshimot num. 39

אלא שהחידושי תורה צריכים להיות לאמיתתה של תורה, ולא חס ושלום לטהר את הטמא כו' ו"לא זכה נעשית לו סם מיתה". והעצה לזה "וה' עמו", שאז "הלכה כמותו בכל מקום".

וזהו "דג שיש לו קשקשת"—תלמיד חכם שהוא ירא שמים—"יש לו סנפיר", שבודאי יחדש ויגלה חלקו בתורה. והוא דג טהור.

The novel interpretations in Torah must be in accordance with the true spirit of Torah, and not, Heaven forbid, a [flawed] effort to purify

Rabbi Menachem Mendel Schneerson
1902–1994

The towering Jewish leader of the 20th century, known as "the Lubavitcher Rebbe," or simply as "the Rebbe." Born in southern Ukraine, the Rebbe escaped Nazi occupied Europe, arriving in the U.S. in June 1941. The Rebbe inspired and guided the revival of traditional Judaism after the European devastation, impacting virtually every Jewish community the world over. The Rebbe often emphasized that the performance of just one additional good deed could usher in the era of Mashiach. The Rebbe's scholarly talks and writings have been printed in more than 200 volumes.

the impure, for "if one is not meritorious, it [Torah] becomes a deathly poison for him." The best way [to ensure one remains loyal to the spirit of Torah] is to have "G-d with him," [i.e., a sense of nullification before G-d] in which case, "the halachah is always in accordance with him."

This, then, is the meaning of the Talmud's statement "All fish that have scales"—i.e., a Torah scholar who has an appropriate measure of fear of Heaven—"have fins"—they will surely produce novel insight in Torah. Such an individual is a "kosher fish."

TEXT 15B

Ibid.

אבל "יש שיש לו סנפיר ואין לו קשקשת"—מחדש בלא יראת שמים, והוא דג טמא.

But, "there are some who have fins and no scales"—there are those who produce novel insights in Torah, but they do not have the proper fear of Heaven. Such a "fish" is not "kosher."

2

MAZRIA–METZORA

In Defense of Consumerism

The Benefits of Owning Lots of Stuff

Student Manual

PARSHA OVERVIEW
Tazria-Metzora

The Parshahs of Tazria and Metzora continue the discussion of the laws of tumah v'taharah, *ritual impurity and purity.*

A woman giving birth should undergo a process of purification, which includes immersing in a mikvah *(a naturally gathered pool of water) and bringing offerings to the Holy Temple. All male infants are to be circumcised on the eighth day of life.*

Tzaraat *(often mistranslated as "leprosy") is a supranatural plague, which can afflict people as well as garments or homes. If white or pink patches appear on a person's skin (dark pink or dark green in garments or homes), a* kohen *is summoned. Judging by various signs, such as an increase in size of the afflicted area after a seven-day quarantine, the* kohen *pronounces it* tamei *(impure) or* tahor *(pure).*

A person afflicted with tzaraat must dwell alone outside of the camp (or city) until he is healed. The afflicted area in a garment or home must be removed; if the tzaraat recurs, the entire garment or home must be destroyed.

When the metzora ("leper") heals, he or she is purified by the kohen with a special procedure involving two birds, spring water in an earthen vessel, a piece of cedar wood, a scarlet thread and a bundle of hyssop.

Ritual impurity is also engendered through a seminal or other discharge in a man, and menstruation or other discharge of blood in a woman, necessitating purification through immersion in a mikvah.

1. The Leprous House

Sparing the House

TEXT 1A

Vayikra 14:33-36

וַיְדַבֵּר ה' אֶל מֹשֶׁה וְאֶל אַהֲרֹן לֵאמֹר:

כִּי תָבֹאוּ אֶל אֶרֶץ כְּנַעַן אֲשֶׁר אֲנִי נֹתֵן לָכֶם לַאֲחֻזָּה וְנָתַתִּי נֶגַע צָרַעַת בְּבֵית אֶרֶץ אֲחֻזַּתְכֶם:

וּבָא אֲשֶׁר לוֹ הַבַּיִת וְהִגִּיד לַכֹּהֵן לֵאמֹר כְּנֶגַע נִרְאָה לִי בַּבָּיִת:

וְצִוָּה הַכֹּהֵן וּפִנּוּ אֶת הַבַּיִת בְּטֶרֶם יָבֹא הַכֹּהֵן לִרְאוֹת אֶת הַנֶּגַע וְלֹא יִטְמָא כָּל אֲשֶׁר בַּבָּיִת וְאַחַר כֵּן יָבֹא הַכֹּהֵן לִרְאוֹת אֶת הַבָּיִת:

And G-d spoke to Moses and to Aaron, saying.

When you come to the land of Canaan, which I am giving you as a possession, and I place a lesion of tzara'at upon a house in the land of your possession.

And the one to whom the house belongs comes and tells the kohen, saying, "Something like a lesion has appeared to me in the house."

The kohen *shall order that they clear out the house, before the* kohen *comes to look at the lesion, so that everything in the house should not become unclean. After this, the* kohen *shall come to look at the house.*

TEXT 1B

Ibid. 14:45-46

וְנָתַץ אֶת הַבַּיִת אֶת אֲבָנָיו וְאֶת עֵצָיו וְאֵת כָּל עֲפַר הַבָּיִת וְהוֹצִיא אֶל מִחוּץ
לָעִיר אֶל מָקוֹם טָמֵא:
וְהַבָּא אֶל הַבַּיִת כָּל יְמֵי הִסְגִּיר אֹתוֹ יִטְמָא עַד הָעָרֶב:

He shall demolish the house, its stones, its wood, and all the [mortar] dust of the house, and he shall take [them] outside the city, to an unclean place.

And anyone entering the house during all the days of its quarantine shall become unclean until the evening.

TEXT 1C

Ibid. 14:48-9, 54-55

וְאִם בֹּא יָבֹא הַכֹּהֵן וְרָאָה וְהִנֵּה לֹא פָשָׂה הַנֶּגַע בַּבַּיִת אַחֲרֵי הִטֹּחַ אֶת הַבָּיִת
וְטִהַר הַכֹּהֵן אֶת הַבַּיִת כִּי נִרְפָּא הַנָּגַע:
וְלָקַח לְחַטֵּא אֶת הַבַּיִת שְׁתֵּי צִפֳּרִים וְעֵץ אֶרֶז וּשְׁנִי תוֹלַעַת וְאֵזֹב:...

But if the kohen comes and comes again and looks [at the lesion], and behold, the lesion did not spread in the house, after the house has been plastered, the kohen shall pronounce the house clean, because the lesion has healed.

To [ritually] cleanse the house, he shall take two birds, a cedar stick, a strip of crimson [wool], and hyssop...

TEXT 2A

Rabbi Shlomo Yitschaki
(Rashi)
1040–1105
Most noted biblical and
Talmudic commentator.
Born in Troyes, France,
Rashi studied in the famed
yeshivot of Mainz and
Worms. His commentaries
on the Pentateuch and the
Talmud, which focus on the
straightforward meaning
of the text, have appeared
in virtually every edition
of the Talmud and Bible.

Rashi Vayikra 14:36

"בטרם יבא הכהן וגו'". שכל זמן שאין כהן נזקק לו, אין שם תורת טומאה.
"ולא יטמא כל אשר בבית". שאם לא יפנהו ויבא הכהן ויראה הנגע,
נזקק להסגר, וכל מה שבתוכו יטמא.
ועל מה חסה תורה, אם על כלי שטף, יטבילם ויטהרו, ואם על אוכלין
ומשקין, יאכלם בימי טומאתו, הא לא חסה התורה אלא על כלי חרס,
שאין להם טהרה במקוה.

"**B**efore the kohen *comes." As long as the* kohen *has not yet become involved with the house [in question], the law of uncleanness does not yet apply to it.*

"So that everything in the house should not become unclean." For if they do not clear it out, and the kohen *comes and sees the lesion, the house will have to be quarantined and everything inside it will become unclean.*

Now, for what objects did the Torah have consideration? If it was upon vessels that require immersion [in a mikvah *to cleanse them], then [instead of having them removed,] let him immerse them, and they will become clean. And if it was upon food and drink, then [instead of removing them, let them become unclean] and he can eat and drink them during his period of uncleanness. Hence, the Torah has consideration only for earthenware vessels, which cannot be cleansed by [immersion in] a* mikvah *[and would thus undergo permanent damage if they became unclean].*

TEXT 2B

Midrash Sifra Metzora 5:12

Sifra
(*Torat Kohanim*)

An ancient rabbinic exegesis on the book of Leviticus. The subject matter of this work is predominately Temple-era-related laws inasmuch as much of the book of Leviticus focuses on the Temple service. According to Maimonides, the compiler and editor of this work was the Talmudic sage Rav (175–247 CE). Others attribute it to an earlier redactor. The work is quoted often in the Talmud.

אמר רבי מאיר... על מה חסה התורה על כלי חרסו ועל פכו וכי מה מטמא בנגעים הרשעים או הצדיקים הוי אומר הרשעים. אם כך חסה תורה על ממונו הבזוי קל וחומר על ממונו החביב! אם כך על ממונו קל וחומר על נפש בניו ובנותיו, אם כך על של רשע קל וחומר על צדיק!

With what was the Torah concerned? —with his earthenware. Now, who is inflicted with tzara'at? —a sinner. If this is how the Torah is concerned with his trivial property, how much more so must it be with his more precious items! If this is how his money [is treated], how much more so must it be regarding the lives of his sons and daughters! If this is how [the Torah regards] that which belongs to a sinner, how much more so with the righteous!

TEXT 3

Rabb Aharon Ibn Chaim, Korban Aharon

"וכי מה מטמא". כלומר, ועוד שאין הרחמנות הזה על הצדיקים שמי הם המיטמאים בנגעים הוי אומר הרשעים ואם כן מכאן נלמוד רחמנות השם יתברך על בריותיו.

G-d's mercy is not extended only to the righteous, for which sort of people contract tzara'at? —sinners. From here we can see the compassion G-d has on His creatures.

2. Mindful Spending

In the Temple

TEXT 4A

Babylonian Talmud
A literary work of monumental proportions that draws upon the legal, spiritual, intellectual, ethical, and historical traditions of Judaism. The 37 tractates of the Babylonian Talmud contain the teachings of the Jewish sages from the period after the destruction of the 2nd Temple through the 5th century CE. It has served as the primary vehicle for the transmission of the Oral Law and the education of Jews over the centuries; it is the entry point for all subsequent legal, ethical, and theological Jewish scholarship.

Talmud Tractate Menachot 76b

תנו רבנן: "סולת ואפית אותה"—מלמד שנקחת סולת. ומנין שאפילו חיטין? תלמוד לומר "ולקחת", מכל מקום... מפני החיסחון. מאי מפני החיסחון? אמר רבי אלעזר: התורה חסה על ממונן של ישראל.

Our Rabbis taught: The verse states [regarding the showbread], *"Fine flour and bake it."* This teaches that fine flour is taken. And how do we know that even grains of wheat may be brought? The text therefore states, *"And you shall take,"* in any manner… to be considerate. What is meant by *"being considerate"*? Said Rabbi Elazar: The Torah is compassionate with the monies of Israel.

TEXT 4B

Rashi ad loc

"לפי שחסה תורה על ממונם של ישראל". לפי שלחם הפנים הם כ"ד עשרונות ולפי שהן בכל שבת ושבת ועולים לדבר גדול הותר לקנותן מן החיטין כדי שיבא לחם בזול יותר משאם היו לוקחין סלת מן התגר שהקונה סלת קונה אותה ביוקר אבל שאר מנחות שהן דבר מועט ואין באות תדיר לא הותרו לקנות כי אם סלת.

"*The Torah is compassionate with the monies of Israel.*" *The showbread contained 24* isaron *[1* isaron *is about 2.4 liters] of flour and were made anew every week—amounting to a very large sum of wheat. Thus, permission was granted to buy it as wheat so that the bread should be cheaper, for ready [fine] flour is expensive. However, the other* menachot *[offerings] were of much smaller quantities and were not offered constantly, and so, it was only permissible to purchase them as ready [fine] wheat.*

TEXT 5

Tractate Rosh Hashanah, 27a

בתעניות בשל זכרים כפופין ופיו מצופה כסף. מאי שנא התם דזהב, ומאי שנא הכא דכסף?... התורה חסה על ממונן של ישראל.

On fast days they used curved shofars *of rams' horns, the mouths of which were overlaid with silver. Why in the other case should gold have been used and here silver? ... The Torah is compassionate with the monies of Israel.*

Other Areas

TEXT 6

The Lubavitcher Rebbe, Likutei Sichot vol. 14 p. 305

לעשות חתונה גדולה ברוחניות ו(על פי רוב זה קשור בקטנות החומריות
והידורי העולם מלשון העלם) מבזבזים ממון—עליו אמרו חכמינו זכרונם
לברכה "התורה חסה על ממונם של ישראל". גדול זכותו וזכות החתן
וכלה שיחיו אם יחזירו תקנת גדולי ישראל בזה לחוגי אנ"ש שיחיו ולכל
בני ישראל שיחיו על ידי הורותם דוגמא חיה בזה ומתוך שמחה וטוב
לבב. ויהא בשעה טובה ומוצלחת.

Rabbi Menachem Mendel Schneerson
1902–1994

The towering Jewish leader of the 20th century, known as "the Lubavitcher Rebbe," or simply as "the Rebbe." Born in southern Ukraine, the Rebbe escaped Nazi occupied Europe, arriving in the U.S. in June 1941. The Rebbe inspired and guided the revival of traditional Judaism after the European devastation, impacting virtually every Jewish community the world over. The Rebbe often emphasized that the performance of just one additional good deed could usher in the era of Mashiach. The Rebbe's scholarly talks and writings have been printed in more than 200 volumes.

You are to make a grand wedding—in a spiritual sense (which, oftentimes, is directly related with decreasing the materialism and worldly extravagance). Wasting money [on material extravagance] is negated by the directive of our Sages, "The Torah is compassionate with the monies of Israel." It would be a great merit for you, as well as for the bride and groom, if you would restore the guidelines of the great Rabbis [regarding minimizing wedding expenditures] to our community and to the Jewish people in general through demonstrating a living example, and with joy and a gladdened heart. The wedding should be in a good and auspicious time.

Easing Up

TEXT 7

Rabbi Shimon ben Tzemach Duran, Zohar Harakia, Introduction §1

במקומות שיש איבוד ממון מחמת ספיקא דרבנן, הדבר הוא יותר
פשוט שהם חייבין להקל בספיקו... באיסורין דרבנן אם אמרו כן להתיר
ספקו, יפה הן עושין שאין לנו לאבד ממונם של ישראל שהוא ודאי
דאורייתא משום ספק דרבנן.

I n a situation where monetary loss will be incurred because of a doubt regarding a rabbinic matter, it is readily understood that the Rabbis must be more lenient in their ruling ... we are lenient with regards to a doubt in rabbinic matters in instances of monetary loss, for we should not be causing Jews monetary loss—which is of definite biblical proportion—for a doubtful matter of rabbinical nature.

Rabbi Shimon ben Tsemach Duran
(Rashbats)
ca. 1361–1444
Physician, poet, rabbi, and philosopher. Duran was a student of philosophy, astronomy, mathematics, and especially of medicine, which he practiced for a number of years in Palma, Spain. He left Spain in the aftermath of the 1391 massacres and moved to Algiers, where, in addition to practicing medicine, he later became the chief rabbi. Among his many works is *Magen* Avot, a philosophical commentary on Tractate Avot.

3. Redeeming Sparks

Optional Section

Vivifying the World

TEXT 8

Rabbi Dovber "the Magid" of Mezeritch
d. 1772

Was the primary disciple and eventual successor of the Ba'al Shem Tov. Amongst his disciples were the founders of various Chasidic dynasties, including Rabbi Nachum of Chernobyl, Rabbi Levi Yitschak of Berditchev, and Rabbi Shne'ur Zalman of Liadi. His teachings, recorded by his students, appear in various volumes including the *Magid Devarav Leya'akov*.

Rabbi Dovber of Mezritch, Ohr Torah, Rimzei Tehillim §233

"הללו את ה' מן השמים". על דרך "לעולם ה' דברך נצב בשמים", על דרך "בדבר ה' שמים נעשו". בהדבור ברא את העולמות, וכח הפועל בנפעל. נמצא כח הדבור הוא בשמים [ועל ידי כח הדבור הזה עומד ויש לו קיום]. וזהו דברך נצב בשמים, הדבור נצב בשמים, רוצה לומר הדבור עומד בשמים ועם זה הדבור מחזיק את השמים.

"**P**raise G-d from the Heavens." This verse conveys a similar idea as the verse "Forever, O Lord, Your word stands in the Heavens," which is similar to the verse "By the word of G-d, the Heavens were made." G-d created the world with His word, investing His energy into creation. Those words stand in the Heavens and sustain the world. This, then, is the meaning of the words, "Your word stands in the Heavens"—namely, the word of G-d is constantly in the Heavens, thereby sustaining them.

End of Optional Section

G-dly Sparks

TEXT 9

Rabbi Chaim Vital, Eitz Chaim 26:1

ואמנם ידעת גם כן כי כל המצות אינם אלא לצרף ולברר הצלם והחומר אך הצורה אין צריך תיקון כלל ולא הוצרכה להתלבש בצלם וחומר רק להמשיך בהם אור לתקנם והבן זה מאד. כי זה טעם ירידת הנשמה בעולם הזה לתקן ולברר דוגמת גלות השכינה לברר ניצוצין שנפלו כנודע.

Rabbi Chaim Vital
ca. 1542–1620

Lurianic Kabbalist. Rabbi Vital was born in Israel, lived in Safed and Jerusalem, and later in Damascus. He was authorized by his teacher, Rabbi Yitschak Luria, the Arizal, to record his teachings. Acting on this mandate, Vital began arranging his master's teachings in written form, and his many works constitute the foundation of the Lurianic school of Jewish mysticism. His most famous work is *Ets Chaim.*

I t is known that the purpose of the mitzvot *is to refine and sublimate the form and the material. The spirit itself does not need refinement, and* the only reason it was enclothed in the form and the material was to draw down a light that would rectify them. For this is the reason the soul descended upon this world—to rectify and to sublimate, similar to the exile of the Shechinah *which is to sublimate the G-dly sparks that have fallen.*

The Secret of Eating

TEXT 10

Rabbi Yisrael Ba'al Shem Tov (Besht)

1698–1760

Founder of the Chasidic movement. Born in Slutsk, Belarus, the Ba'al Shem Tov was orphaned as a child. He served as a teacher's assistant and clay digger before founding the Chasidic movement and revolutionizing the Jewish world with his emphasis on prayer, joy, and love for every Jew, regardless of his or her level of Torah knowledge.

Rabbi Yisrael Ba'al Shem Tov, Keter Shem Tov §194

והמשל למלך שנאבדה לו אבן טוב מתוך טבעתו, והנה עמדו לפני המלך בעת ההיא הרבה מעבדיו ושריו הפרתמים והפחות והסגנים מאנשי מלחמתו עד אין מספר, עם כל זה לא רצה המלך לצוות להם שיחפשו אחר האבן טוב, רק צוה לבנו יחידו וחביבו שיחפש וימצא האבידה ויחזירנה לאביו המלך, הגם שהיה המלך בטוח מכל אחד משריו ועבדיו שכאשר ימצאנו יחזירנו בשלימות, אף על פי כן לא היה ברצונו שהם יחפשו כי רצה לזכות את בנו חביבו וכדי שיקרא המציאה על שמו. ולא עוד, אלא גם רמז לבנו חביבו בכמה רמזים מציאותו, כי מתחלה היתה האבידה מדעת המלך את מקומה ועשה הכל רק למען לזכות את בנו חביבו, וכדי שיגיע גם להמלך מזה גודל שעשוע והתפארות מבנו לאמר ראו כי שום בן אדם בעולם לא היה יכול לחפוש ולמצוא זולת בנו חביבו. והנמשל מובן, שתחילת בריאת העולמות היה כדי לברר הניצוצין קדישין על ידי אומה ישראלית, כמו שנאמר "בשביל ישראל שנקרא ראשית", שעל ידם יבררו ממאכלים מותרים וכשרים.

וזהו שאמר ר' ישראל בעל שם על פסוק "רעבים גם צמאים נפשם בהם תתעטף", פירוש בכאן סוד גדול [ונורא], והוא למה ברא הקדוש ברוך הוא דברי מאכל ומשקה שאדם תאב להם [לאכול ולשתות]? והטעם שהם [ממש ניצוצות אדם הראשון שהם] מתלבשים בדומם צומח חי מדבר ויש להם חשק להדבק בקדושה, והם מעוררים מיין נוקבין בסוד אין טפה יורדה מלמעלה שאין טפיים עולים כנגדה, וכל אכילה [ושתיה] שאדם אוכל ושותה היא ממש חלק ניצוצות שלו שהוא צריך לתקן. וזהו שכתוב "רעבים גם צמאים", כשאדם רעב וצמא להם, למה זה, [וזהו שכתוב] "נפשם בהם תתעטף", בסוד גלות [בלבושי

זרים] ויחשבה לזונה כי כסתה פניה, וכל הדברים שהם משמשין לאדם הם ממש בסוד הבני' שלו שהלבישו, והבן.

והשם יתברך רמז להם לישראל בכמה רמזים שימצאו האבידה ויחזרו לבעליהם, לאביהם שבשמים, ולא צוה כן למלאכים ושרפים ואופנים, והאבידה ההוא מדעת היתה כמאמר רז"ל שהיה בונה עולמות ומחריבן.

An analogy:

A king once lost a precious stone. All the important ministers, aides, officers, and military leaders were present, yet the king did not instruct them to find his precious stone, rather he directed his instruction to his beloved only son. Though the king had complete confidence that his ministers and servants could surely find the stone and faithfully return it, he wished to bestow his beloved son with the great honor of being the one who successfully found the lost item. What's more, the truth is that the king really knew where the stone was hidden, and he engineered the whole ploy just to give his beloved son more opportunity and so that he should enjoy the immense pleasure of seeing his own son be the only one to find the stone. So, he even hinted to his son where the stone may be found.

The analog is obvious: The entire purpose of why G-d created this world was so that the Jews could redeem the G-dly sparks, for the Jew can sublimate kosher and permissible food items.

The Baal Shem Tov revealed a fascinating secret hidden in the words of the verse, "Hungry as well as thirsty, their soul enwraps itself in them." These words come to answer the question, "Why did G-d create food items that man craves and needs to survive?"

The reason is that the divine sparks of G-d are trapped in the various creations on earth. These sparks wish to cleave to holiness, so they call out and stir a response. Every time a person eats or drinks, he is sublimating these sparks that have called out and need refinement. This, then, is the meaning of the verse, "Hungry as well as thirsty, their soul enwraps itself in them"—why is a person hungry or thirsty for food and drink? "Because of the soul that is trapped within them."

G-d hints to the Jew in various ways to find the lost object and return it to its rightful owner—their Father in Heaven. [As in the analogy,] G-d did not instruct the angels, and the loss was intentional.

Hang on to it!

TEXT 11

Rabbi Zvi Elimelech Shapiro of Dinov, Bnei Yissaschar,
Ma'amarei Chodesh Adar, Ma'amar 2, Shekel Hakodesh §7

למה תהיה כזאת, שלפעמים תתבטל חתיכת איסור בהיתר והוא נאכל על פי התורה, כגון שנתבטל בששים או יבש ביבש ברוב?

תדע, שהוא ממחשבות הצור תם. הוא יתברך שמו יודע אשר הניצוץ הטמון באותה חתיכה האסורה ביחוד, יכול להתברר על ידינו. הנה השם

יתברך מזמין שתיפול החתיכה האסורה כזאת לתוך היתר, ותתבטל,
ואכול יאכלו אותה על פי התורה, ותתברר הניצוץ הזה וכו'. ואם כן,
מצוה היא בדווקא שיאכל הישראלי החתיכה ההוא, ולא יחמיר וכו'.
על כן, לדעתי הצעירה, אין זה מדרך החסידות מה שכמה אנשים נוהגים
סלסול בעצמם, שלא לאכול משום מאכל שהיה עליו שאלת חכם, הגם
שהוא דבר פשוט ומבואר דינו להיתר, כגון על ידי תערובת בששים
וכיוצא בזה.

W*hy does it happen that sometimes, forbidden matter will fall into permissible matter and become permissible, like a one in sixty?*

Know that this is G-d's plan. He knows that there is a G-dly spark hidden in that forbidden item that can be redeemed. So, He orchestrates that it should mix with permissible matter and be eaten in accordance to the Torah law—thus redeeming that spark. It follows that it is a great mitzvah to eat that item, and one should not be needlessly stringent.

Accordingly, in my humble opinion, if there are clear halachic *grounds to permit a questionable food item, one should not abstain from it; those who do are not considered pious at all.*

Rabbi Tzvi Elimelech Schapiro
(*Benei Yisaschar*)
1783–1841
Rabbi Schapiro was the student of Rabbi Ya'akov Yitschak of Lublin and of his uncle, Rabbi Elimelech of Lizhensk. He was influential in bringing the Chasidic movement to Galician and Hungarian Jewry. He authored *Benei Yisaschar*. His descendants established the Chasidic dynasties of Dinov, Munkach, and Bluzhov.

4. Your Personal Chance

Your Possessions

TEXT 12

Rabbi Dovber of Mezritch, Ohr Torah, Agaddot Chazal §413

התורה חסה על ממונם של ישראל. ולמה כך, כי זה כלל גדול שכל
דבר שאדם לובש או אוכל או משתמש בכלי, הוא נהנה מהחיות שיש
באותו דבר. כי לולי אותו הרוחניות לא היה שום קיום לאותו דבר, ויש
שם ניצוצות קדושות השייכים לשורש נשמתו. (ושמעתי כי זהו הטעם
שיש אדם שאוהב דבר זה, ויש אדם ששונא דבר זה ואוהב דבר אחר.)
וכשהוא משתמש באותו הכלי, או אוכל מאכל אפילו לצורך גופו, הוא
מתקן הניצוצין. כי אחר כך עובד בכח הזה שבא לגופו מאותו מלבוש או
מאכל או שאר דברים, ובזה הכח עובד להשם יתברך, נמצאו מתוקנים.
ולכך פעמים שיאבד הדבר ההוא ממנו. שכבר כלה לתקן כל הניצוצין
שהיו באותו הדבר השייכין לשורש נשמתו, אז לוקח ממנו השם יתברך
אותו הכלי ונותן לאחר ששייכין הניצוצות שיש באותו הכלי לשורש
[של] אחר [שהוא משורש נשמתו.]...
לכך צריך אדם לחוס על כליו ועל כל דבר שיש לו, דהיינו מצד הניצוצין
שיש שם, בכדי לחוס על הניצוצין הקדושות.

The Torah is compassionate with the monies of Israel. Why is this so? Know this broad rule: A person derives benefit from the energy contained within every item he eats, wears, or otherwise uses. Were it not for that spiritual energy, it would not exist. Now, there are holy sparks in that item that relate exclusively with the soul of its owner, and when he or she uses or eats that item—even if only for bodily purposes—they redeem those sparks. For afterward, he or she serves G-d with those garments or with the energy from that food, thus sublimating the sparks trapped inside of them.

[I have heard that this is the reason why some people like certain items and despise others, while other people like those same items and despise different ones.]

For this reason, people will lose their money or personal articles. The owner has finished redeeming the sparks in that item which relate exclusively to his soul, so G-d takes it away and gives it to another person whose soul **does** relate to the remaining sparks in that item...

One must therefore be careful with his personal articles and possessions, that is, he should be mindful of the divine sparks hidden inside them.

TEXT 13

The Lubavitcher Rebbe, Torat Menachem vol. 27 173

כיון ש"לא ברא הקדוש ברוך הוא דבר אחד לבטלה", ניתן לכל אחד מישראל מספר מסויים של כחות ועניינים כדי שיוכל למלא שליחותו בעלמא דין, ולכן, כאשר מנצל אחד מעניניו שלא לצורך מילוי שליחותו, הרי לא זו בלבד שעושה דבר שאין לו תוכן, אלא עוד זאת, שחסר לו

השעה, העניין והכח (המשכת הנפש) שהיה צריך לנצל כדי לפעול בעניין של תורה ומצוות

וזהו גם תוכן העניין ש"התורה חסה על ממונם של ישראל", כמבואר בתורת החסידות תורת הבעל שם טוב והרב המגיד, ש"יש שם ניצוצין קדושים השייכים לשורש נשמתו, וכשהוא משתמש באותו הכלי . . הוא מתקן הניצוצין . . לכך צריך אדם לחוס על כליו ועל כל דבר שיש לו כו'".

והעניין בזה:

כאשר דבר מסויים נמצא ברשותו של יהודי, הרי זה סימן שדבר זה שייך אליו, לתכלית בריאתו–"אני נבראתי לשמש את קוני", שזהו עניין שעל ידו צריך למלא שליחותו.

וכיון שכן, הרי "התורה חסה על ממונם של ישראל" ... כיון שיש בו ניצוץ קדושה שצריך לברר ולזכך ולהעלות ולקשר עם אלקות, ואם דבר זה הולך לאיבוד, אזי חסר לו חלק בעבודתו.

ומזה מובן שכל עשיותיו של האדם צריכים להיות עניין של קדושה – שזהו תוכן פסק דין הרמב"ם "צריך האדם שיכוון לבו וכל מעשיו כולם לידע את השם ברוך הוא בלבד . . נמצא המהלך בדרך זו כל ימיו עובד את ה' תמיד . . בכל דרכיך דעהו".

Because "G-d did not create anything need-lessly," it follows that every person is given a certain amount of capability to fulfill his or her mission on earth. When he uses these capabilities for something other than his life's mission, it's not just that he's doing something meaningless—he is now lacking the time, the energy, and the spirit that was supposed to be used to fulfill a meaningful act of Torah and mitzvot.

This is the idea behind the words, "The Torah is compassionate with the monies of Israel," as is explained by the Baal Shem Tov and the Maggid: There are holy sparks in that item that relate specifically to the soul of its owner, and when he or she utilizes that item... they redeem those sparks... One must therefore be careful with his personal articles and possessions.

To explain:

When certain things wind up in the possession of a Jew, it is a divine sign that the particular item is relevant to him and his raison d'être—to serve G-d: This is an item that must be utilized to fulfill his mission.

Accordingly, the Torah is mindful of a Jew's possessions... because there is a divine spark that the owner must refine and redeem and bring to G-d; if the item were to be lost or destroyed, the owner would then be missing a part of his mission.

From the above we can understand that one's every action should be imbued with a sense of holiness, pointed towards the service of G-d.

With Mitzvot

TEXT 14

The Lubavitcher Rebbe, Likutei Sichot vol. 18 p. 225

ויש לומר בדרך אפשר—אז דאס גופא איז דער טעם וואס סיי ביי
מתנות כהונה סיי בא מעשר איז דא שיעור א קצוב, און א מענטש טאר
ניט אוועקגעבן זיינע גאנצע נכסים—ווארום די פארבונדנקייט מיט
אלקות אין די נכסים איז אין א אנדער אופן ווי אין די וואס ער דארף
אוועקגעבן; און דעריבער איז "חסה התורה על ממונם של ישראל" (כדי
זיי זאלן נתברר ווערן אויף זייער ריכטיקן אופן).

he Priestly gifts and the tithes are limited, and
a person is actually not allowed to give away
all of his possessions. The reason for this is
because the connection with G-d designed for a man's
personal possessions is different from the connection
designed for the items that fall under compulsory tithing and giving. Accordingly, "The Torah was compassionate for the monies of Israel" so that the remaining
personal items should be sublimated in the manner
appropriate for **them** [through their owner].

3

ACHAREI-KEDOSHIM

When No Means Go

How Limits Help Us Go Further in Life

Student Manual

PARSHA OVERVIEW
Acharei-Kedoshim

Following the deaths of Nadav and Avihu, G-d warns against unauthorized entry "into the holy." Only one person, the kohen gadol ("high priest"), may—but once a year, on Yom Kippur—enter the innermost chamberin the Sanctuary to offer the sacred ketoret to G-d.

Another feature of the Day of Atonement service is the casting of lots over two goats, to determine which should be offered to G-d and which should be dispatched to carry off the sins of Israel to the wilderness.

The Parshah of Acharei also warns against bringing korbanot (animal or meal offerings) anywhere but in the Holy Temple, forbids the consumption of blood, and details the laws prohibiting incest and other deviant sexual relations.

The Parshah of Kedoshim begins with the statement: "You shall be holy, for I, the L-rd your G-d, am holy." This is followed by dozens of mitzvot (divine commandments) through which the Jew sanctifies him- or herself and relates to the holiness of G-d.

These include: the prohibition against idolatry, the mitzvah of charity, the principle of equality before the law, Shabbat, sexual morality, honesty in business, honor and awe of one's parents, and the sacredness of life.

Also in Kedoshim is the dictum which the great sage Rabbi Akiva called a cardinal principle of Torah, and of which Hillel said, "This is the entire Torah, the rest is commentary"—"Love your fellow as yourself."

1. Questionable Behavior

Love Your Neighbor

TEXT 1A

Vayikra 19:18

לֹא תִקֹּם וְלֹא תִטֹּר אֶת בְּנֵי עַמֶּךָ וְאָהַבְתָּ לְרֵעֲךָ כָּמוֹךָ אֲנִי ה':

You shall neither take revenge from, nor bear a grudge against, the members of your people; you shall love your neighbor as yourself. I am G-d.

TEXT 1B

Rabbi Shlomo Yitschaki
(Rashi)
1040–1105

Most noted biblical and Talmudic commentator. Born in Troyes, France, Rashi studied in the famed *yeshivot* of Mainz and Worms. His commentaries on the Pentateuch and the Talmud, which focus on the straightforward meaning of the text, have appeared in virtually every edition of the Talmud and Bible.

Rashi ad loc.

"ואהבת לרעך כמוך". אמר רבי עקיבא זה כלל גדול בתורה.

"You shall love your neighbor as yourself." Rabbi Akiva says, "This is a fundamental principle of the Torah."

Shammai's Stick

TEXT 2

Talmud Tractate Shabbat 31a

שוב מעשה בנכרי אחד שבא לפני שמאי, אמר לו "גיירני על מנת
שתתלמדני כל התורה כולה כשאני עומד על רגל אחת". דחפו באמת
הבנין שבידו.

בא לפני הלל, גייריה. אמר לו "דעלך סני לחברך לא תעביד, זו היא כל
התורה כולה; ואידך, פירושה הוא, זיל גמור".

Babylonian Talmud
A literary work of monumental proportions that draws upon the legal, spiritual, intellectual, ethical, and historical traditions of Judaism. The 37 tractates of the Babylonian Talmud contain the teachings of the Jewish sages from the period after the destruction of the 2nd Temple through the 5th century CE. It has served as the primary vehicle for the transmission of the Oral Law and the education of Jews over the centuries; it is the entry point for all subsequent legal, ethical, and theological Jewish scholarship.

A gentile once came before Shammai and said, "Convert me to Judaism, on the stipulation that you teach me the entire Torah as I stand on one leg." Shammai drove him off with the builder's measuring stick which was in his hand.

He then came before Hillel, who converted him, telling him: "What is hateful to you, do not do to your fellow. This is the entire Torah. The rest is commentary—go and learn."

Stern Shammai

TEXT 3

Mishnah
The first authoritative work of Jewish law that was codified in writing. The Mishnah contains the oral traditions that were passed down from teacher to student; it supplements, clarifies, and systematizes the commandments of the Torah. Due to the continual persecution of the Jewish people, it became increasingly difficult to guarantee that these traditions would not be forgotten. Rabbi Yehudah Hanasi therefore redacted the Mishnah at the end of the 2nd century. It serves as the foundation for the Talmud.

Mishnah Tractate Eduyot 4:1

אלו דברים מקולי בית שמאי ומחומרי בית הלל...

These are the items where the school of Shammai is more lenient while the school of Hillel is more stringent...

TEXT 4

Talmud Tractate Shabbat 30b

תנו רבנן: לעולם יהא אדם ענוותן כהלל ואל יהא קפדן כשמאי.

Our Rabbis taught: One should always be gentle like Hillel, and not stern like Shammai.

Different Souls

TEXT 5

Rabbi Shneur Zalman of Liadi, Tanya Igeret Hakodesh ch. 13

Rabbi Shneur Zalman of Liadi
(Alter Rebbe)
1745–1812

Chasidic rebbe, halachic authority, and founder of the Chabad movement. The Alter Rebbe was born in Liozna, Belarus, and was among the principal students of the Magid of Mezeritch. His numerous works include the *Tanya*, an early classic containing the fundamentals of Chabad Chasidism, and *Shulchan Aruch HaRav*, a code of Jewish law.

הנה בכלל עובדי השם יש ב' בחינות ומדרגות חלוקות מצד שורש נשמתם למעלה מבחינת ימין ושמאל דהיינו שבחינת שמאל היא מדת הצמצום וההסתר בעבודת השם... ממדה זו נמשכה גם כן בחינת הצמצום והגבול בעבודת ה' כמו בצדקה להיות נידון בהשג יד והמבזבז אל יבזבז יותר מחומש וכהאי גוונא בתלמוד תורה ושארי מצות די לו שיוצא ידי חובתו מחויב מפורש שחייבתו התורה בפירוש לקבוע עתים כו'.

אך בחינת ימין היא מדת החסד וההתפשטות בעבודת ה' בהתרחבות בלי צמצום והסתר כלל... וגם בלי צמצום וגבול כלל ואין מעצור לרוח נדבתו בין בצדקה ובין בתלמוד תורה ושארי מצות ולא די לו לצאת ידי חובתו בלבד...

בית שמאי ששרש נשמתם מבחינת שמאל העליון ולכן היו דנין להחמיר תמיד בכל איסורי התורה. ובית הלל שהיו מבחינת ימין העליון היו מלמדין זכות להקל.

Among those who serve G-d, there are two degrees and levels which, depending on the root of their souls above, are distinct in relation to the categories of the right and the left. The characteristic of the left is the trait of constraint and concealment in the service of G-d… This attribute lends to constraint and limitation in Divine service; for example, with regards to charity—to judge according to the means. Similarly, with regards to Torah study and the other commandments—such a person suffices *in discharging his duty, namely the definite duty to which the Torah obliges him…*

Contrarily, the characteristic of the right is the attribute of grace and expanse in Divine service, without any constraint and concealment at all… There is no restraint to the spirit of his generosity—whether it be with respect to charity, Torah study, or other commandments. He does not suffice in discharging his obligation only…

The souls of Bet Shammai were rooted in the pristine Supernal Left. This explains why Bet Shammai consistently ruled stringently regarding all the prohibitions of the Torah. Contrarily, Bet Hillel, who were of the Supernal Right, would find favorable arguments to be lenient.

Question—This Is Called Welcoming?

TEXT 6

Mishnah Tractate Avot 1:15

שמאי אומר, "עשה תורתך קבע, אמור מעט ועשה הרבה; והוי מקביל את כל האדם, בסבר פנים יפות".

Shammai would say: Make your Torah study a permanent fixture of your life. Say little and do much. And receive every man with a pleasant countenance.

2. Understanding Shammai

Only with Proper Respect

TEXT 7

Rabbi Dovid Pardo
1718–1790

Italian Rabbi and liturgical poet, born in Veince and lived for some time in Sarajevo, eventually assuming the position as the city's chief Rabbi. Towards the end of his life, he immigrated to Jerusalem and died there. Among other things, he authored a commentary on the Sifra on Leviticus and Maskil Ledavid, a super-commentary on Rashi on the Torah.

Rabbi Dovid Pardo, Shoshanim Le'dovid, Shabbat ad loc.

אדם לא קאמר אלא האדם הידוע, דהיינו כשבא לפניך בהשכל, דאם לא כן, אלא שבא בשגעון כמו אותו נכרי שבא לפני שמאי ואמר גיירני על מנת שאהיה כהן גדול וכו' שאז סבירא ליה לשמאי שאין לקבלו, כנראה משם שדחפו באמת הבנין כנזכר לעיל כי היכי דלא תיקשי מדידיה אדידיה, או שלא יאמר המתעקש שהיה נאה דורש ואין נאה מקיים חלילה.

Shammai does not use the word "man," rather "the man," namely a person who approaches you in a reasonable manner. If this is not the case, rather he approaches with absurdities—like the gentile who approached Shammai and asked to convert on condition that he become the High Priest [a similar story quoted in the same passage]—in such a scenario, Shammai would assert that he is not to be received graciously. Shammai indeed reacted that way, pushing the convert away with a builder's stick.

As such, it is reasonable to assume that Shammai's behavior is not self-contradictory—to preempt the *pesky ones who will claim that Shammai was good at preaching but not in practice.*

TEXT 8

Rabbi Shmuel di Azouda, Midrash Shmuel, Avot ad loc.

או יאמר "והוי מקבל את כל האדם" ולא אמר "את כל העולם", כלומר מי שהוא במדריגת אדם וישאל שאלת אדם. אבל כשישאל שאלת נבלים, אין לחוש ממנו, וכמו שאמר הכתוב "אל תען כסיל כאולתו".

Rabbi Shmuel di Azouda
1545–1604
Commentator and Preacher. Rabbi Azouda was born in the famed city of Safed and was a disciple of the Arizal and Rabbi Chaim Vital, with whom he studied Kabbalah. He became a rabbi and preacher in Safed and later in Constantinople. Rabbi Arma'ah authored a number of works, and is best known as the author of Midrash Shmuel, a compendium of commentaries on Tractate Avot that has since been widely received as the authoritative commentary on this tract.

The Mishnah specifically states, "And receive every man with a pleasant countenance," and not "the entire world." The implication is that the individual must be acting as a respectable human being, asking respectful questions. But when the individual asks the questions of villains, one need not take concern, as the verse states, "Do not answer a fool according to his folly."

Learning from the Best

TEXT 9

Rabbi Menachem Mendel Schneerson
1902–1994

The towering Jewish leader of the 20th century, known as "the Lubavitcher Rebbe," or simply as "the Rebbe." Born in southern Ukraine, the Rebbe escaped Nazi occupied Europe, arriving in the U.S. in June 1941. The Rebbe inspired and guided the revival of traditional Judaism after the European devastation, impacting virtually every Jewish community the world over. The Rebbe often emphasized that the performance of just one additional good deed could usher in the era of Mashiach. The Rebbe's scholarly talks and writings have been printed in more than 200 volumes.

The Lubavitcher Rebbe, Likutei Sichot vol. 17 p. 114-115 fn. 37

יש לבאר במאמר שמאי ... "הוי מקבל את כל האדם בסבר פנים יפות", אף שמצינו שהנהגתו היתה באופן הפכי בהנכרים שבאו להתגייר אצלו... אלא—לאחר שאמר הלל "הוי מתלמידיו של אהרן אוהב שלום" פעל גם על שמאי שהיה מבחינת הגבורות שגם הוא יאמר "והוי מקבל את כל האדם בסבר פנים יפות, אף שמצד עצמו "דחפו באמת הבנין".

Shammai's statement, *"And receive every man with a pleasant countenance,"* requires explanation in light of his contrary behavior with the prospective convert who approached him.

It can be suggested that Hillel's teaching, "One should be of the students of Aaron, lovers of peace," impacted Shammai to the extent that though he personally [possessed a soul stemming] from the Supernal Severities and had the tendency to push people away, he turned around and stated "and receive every man with a pleasant countenance."

Falling to Lift Another

TEXT 10A

Rabbi Dovber, the Maggid of Mezeritch, Ohr Torah p. 451

Rabbi Dovber "the Magid" of Mezeritch
d. 1772
Was the primary disciple and eventual successor of the Ba'al Shem Tov. Amongst his disciples were the founders of various Chasidic dynasties, including Rabbi Nachum of Chernobyl, Rabbi Levi Yitschak of Berditchev, and Rabbi Shne'ur Zalman of Liadi. His teachings, recorded by his students, appear in various volumes including the *Magid Devarav Leya'akov*.

ויש לפרש על פי מה שאמר רבותינו זכרונם לברכה "לא הגלה הקדוש ברוך הוא את ישראל אלא להוסיף עליהם גרים". כי הצדיק רוצה להיות במדריגה שלו תמיד, כי הוא רוצה להיות תמיד בפני אדוניו לשרתו.

אך מפני מה הוא נופל לפעמים ממדריגתו? כדי לברר ניצוצין שנפלו בקליפות.

כמשל המלך ששלח את בנו להביא אליו אוצר שנאבד לו, וציוה להביאה [לו] ממדינה אחרת. אם כן מוכרח הבן להחליף מלבושיו כדי שלא יכירוהו. וכן עשה, והביא לו את האוצר, ואז הוא עובד יותר למלך בזה מקודם שהיה עומד לפני המלך. והם נקראים גרים כידוע.

וזהו הפירוש שאמר הגר שילמוד את כל התורה כשהוא עומד על רגל אחד, רצה לומר על מדריגה אחת והעמדה אחת, דחפוהו באמת הבנין, הוא ז' ימי הבנין. כי בכל אחד יש בוקר וערב, וטוב ורע, אם כן צריך הצדיק לירד ממדריגתו לפעמים בכדי לברר ניצוצות אלו שנפלו בקליפות.

We can explain the story with Shammai based on the statement of our Sages, "G-d only exiled the Jews in order to increase converts." The tzadik constantly wants to be on his high spiritual level as he always wants to be in the presence of his Master to serve Him.

Why, indeed, is it that he sometimes falls from his high spiritual level? It is so that he can refine the Divine sparks that have fallen into the evil of kelipot.

A parable: There was a king who sent his son to another [hostile] country to recapture a treasure that had been lost. The son was forced to disguise himself in different clothes so that the townspeople would not recognize him. He disguised himself and was able to return with the treasure. The son was then closer to his father, the king, more so than before. [Similarly, the tzaddik must fall from his lofty level and descend into a new form in order to sublimate the sparks.] These sparks are called "converts," as it is known.

This is the explanation to the words of the convert who asked for the entire Torah to be taught to him as he stood on one foot. "Standing on one foot" means remaining on one stable, spiritual level. "Thereupon he repulsed him with the builder's cubit..." This represents "the seven days of building," [the six days of creation and Shabbos], because within each of the seven days there is [as the Torah spells out] morning and evening, representing good and bad.

Therefore, sometimes the tzadik needs to descend from his level in order to refine these sparks that have fallen in the evil of kelipot.

Don't do it to Someone Else

TEXT 10B

Ibid.

והלל אמר לו "מה דעלך סני לחברך לא תעביד". פירוש אלו לא נפל
הצדיק ממדריגה שלו לא היה [לך] עלייה, [ואם כן מה דעלך סני] לחברך
נמי לא תעביד.

Hillel [further explained the message of Shammai and] said to him, "What is hateful to you, do not do to your neighbor." Meaning, if the tzadik would not descend from his level, you—who are of lesser stature—would have never been elevated. Therefore, what is hateful to you, do not do your neighbor. [Do not demand to always retain a lofty standing, for you were only elevated because a tzadik has descended from his level.]

3. The "Yes" and the "No"

The Two Pillars of Judaism

TEXT 11

Tanya, ch. 20

והנה מודעת זאת לכל כי מצות ואזהרת עבודה זרה שהם שני דברות הראשונים "אנכי" ו"לא יהיה לך" הם כללות כל התורה כולה. כי דבור אנכי כולל כל רמ"ח מצות עשה. ולא יהיה לך כולל כל שס"ה מצות לא תעשה. ולכן שמענו "אנכי" ו"לא יהיה לך" לבד מפי הגבורה כמאמר רבותינו זכרונם לברכה, מפני שהם כללות התורה כולה.

It is well known that the commandment and admonition concerning idolatry, which are contained in the first two commandments of the Decalogue— "I am the Lord your G-d" and "You shall not have any other gods," comprise the entire Torah. For the commandment "I am" encompasses all of the 248 positive precepts, whereas the commandment "You shall not have" encompasses all of the 365 prohibitions. That is why we heard only "I am" and "You shall not have" directly from the Almighty [as opposed to the others which were transmitted by Moshe] as our Sages say, because these two are the sum total of the entire Torah.

Borders Built of Roses

TEXT 12

Shir Hashirim (Song of Songs) 7:3

שָׁרְרֵךְ אַגַּן הַסַּהַר אַל יֶחְסַר הַמָּזֶג בִּטְנֵךְ עֲרֵמַת חִטִּים סוּגָה בַּשּׁוֹשַׁנִּים.

Your navel is [like] a round basin, where no mixed wine is lacking; your belly is [like] a stack of wheat, fenced in with roses.

TEXT 13A

Midrash Shir Hashirim Rabah 7:3

"סוגה בשושנים" אלו דברי תורה שהן רכים כשושנים... אמר רבי לוי, בנוהג שבעולם אדם נושא אשה בן ל' שנה בן מ' שנה. משמוציא יציאותיו הוא בא לזקק לה, והיא אומרת לו "כשושנה אדומה ראיתי" ופורש ממנה מיד. מי גרם לו שלא יקרב לה? איזה כותל ברזל יש ביניהם? ואיזה עמוד ברזל ביניהם? אי זה נחש נשכו? איזה עקרב עקצו שלא יקרב לה? דברי תורה שרכין כשושנה! שנאמר בה "ואל אשה בנדת טומאתה לא תקרב".

וכן מי שהביאו לו תמחוי של חתיכות, אמרו לו חלב נפל שם, ומשך ידו ולא טעמו. מי גרם לו שלא לטעום? איזה נחש נשכו שלא יטעום? ואיזה עקרב עקצו שלא יקרב ויטעם אותו? דברי תורה שרכין כשושנה! שכתוב בה "כל חלב וכל דם לא תאכלו".

Shir Hashirim Rabah
A Midrashic text and exegetical commentary on the book of Song of Songs. This Midrash explicates this biblical book based on the principle that its verses convey an allegory of the relationship between G-d and the people of Israel. It was compiled and edited in the land of Israel during the 6th century.

"Fenced in with roses" refers to words of Torah which are as soft as roses...

Rabbi Levi said: When a Jewish man marries a woman, at the age of 30 or 40, after spending much money on the wedding he finally wants to consummate the marriage. She tells him, "I saw an emission of [menstrual] blood as red as a rose," and he immediately separates from [intimacy with] her [as the law of family purity requires]. Who caused him to separate? Is there a wall of iron between them? Is there a steel pillar? Did a snake threaten to bite him? A scorpion? Why will he not approach her? It is only the words of Torah that are as soft as a rose which states, "Do not approach a woman in the impurity of her period."

Likewise, if one is brought a dish of meat, but then is told "forbidden fats fell into this," he refrains and does not eat it. Who caused him to do this? Did a snake threaten to bite him? Did a scorpion prevent him from eating it? No! It is only the words of Torah that are as soft as roses which state, "Do not eat [forbidden] fats or blood."

TEXT 13B

Rashi, ad loc.

"סוגה בשושנים". גדורה ומסוייגת בגדר שושנים, די לה בגדר קל ואין אחד מכם פורץ בו ליכנס. הרי חתן נכנס לחופה, לבו מגעגעת לחופה ולחיבת חתוניו, בא ליזקק לה, אמרה לו טיפת דם כחרדל ראיתי, הרי הופך פניו לצד אחר ולא נשכו נחש ולא עקרב עוקצו. הרי שהוא עובר בדרך ראה בכורות בראשי התאנים, פשט ידו ליטול, אומרים לו של ישראל הם, הוא מושך ידו מפני הגזל. הרי סוגה בשושנים.

"**F**enced in with roses." Fenced and hedged about with roses. A light fence suffices, and no one breaches it to enter.

For example, a bridegroom enters the nuptial canopy, his heart longing for the nuptials and for the love of his marriage. When he comes to consummate the marriage, she says to him, "I have perceived a drop of blood like [the size of] a mustard seed." He turns his face the other way. Now no snake bit him, nor did a scorpion sting him.

[Similarly,] one passes by on the road and sees freshly ripened fruit at the top of the fig trees. He stretches out his hand to take [them]. They tell him, "These belong to owners," and he withdraws his hand because of [the prohibition] of theft. This is the meaning of "she is fenced in with roses."

Shammai's Roses

TEXT 14

The Lubavitcher Rebbe, Torat Menachem 5745 vol. 4 p. 2122

דחייתו של שמאי גרמה להם לבוא ל"הלל", וכתוצאה מזה לקבל את ב'
הקוין ואופני העבודה דשמאי והלל: קו העבודה דשמאי—"סור מרע",
וקו העבודה דהלל—"עשה טוב". ונמצא, שדחיה זו עצמה יש בה ענין
של "סבר פנים יפות"—לזכותם בב' הקוין דסור מרע ועשה טוב, מצוות
עשה ומצוות לא תעשה, שכללותם—ב' דברות הראשונות "אנכי" ו"לא
יהיה לך".

Shammai's rejection compelled the gentile to seek Hillel, and collectively, he received the two dynamics and methods of service embodied through Shammai and Hillel—Shammai's path of "abstaining from evil" and Hillel's path of "doing good."

It turns out that Shammai's very rejection contained an element of graciousness in the sense that it bestowed upon the gentile the element of "abstaining from evil" in addition to "doing good." [These two ideas are quite central, in that they are the basis for] all positive and negative commandments, which collectively fall under the umbrella commandments of "I am the Lord your G-d" and "You shall have no other gods."

4

LAG BAOMER

The 49-Step Program

Sefirah's Seven-Week Plan for Personal Reform

Student Manual

PARSHA OVERVIEW
Lag Baomer

Lag BaOmer, the 33rd day of the Omer count is a festive day on the Jewish calendar. It is celebrated with outings (on which the children traditionally play with bows and arrows), bonfires, and other joyous events. Many visit the resting place (in Meron, northern Israel) of the great sage and mystic Rabbi Shimon bar Yochai, the anniversary of whose passing is on this day.

Rabbi Shimon bar Yochai, who lived in the second century of the common era, was the first to publicly teach the mystical dimension of the Torah known as the "Kabbalah," and is the author of the basic work of Kabbalah, the Zohar. On the day of his passing, Rabbi Shimon instructed his disciples to mark the date as "the day of my joy."

The chassidic masters explain that the final day of a righteous person's earthly life marks the point at which "all his deeds, teachings and work" achieve their culminating perfection and the zenith of their impact upon our lives. So each Lag BaOmer, we celebrate Rabbi Shimon's life and the revelation of the esoteric soul of Torah.

Lag BaOmer also commemorates another joyous event. The Talmud relates that in the weeks between the Jewish holidays of Passover and Shavuot, a plague raged amongst the disciples of the great sage Rabbi Akiva, "because they did not act respectfully towards each other." These weeks are therefore observed as a period of mourning, with various joyous activities proscribed by law and custom. On Lag BaOmer the deaths ceased. Thus, Lag BaOmer also carries the theme of the imperative to love and respect one's fellow (ahavat yisrael).

1. Sefiras Haomer

The Omer Offering

TEXT 1

Vayikra 23:10

דַּבֵּר אֶל בְּנֵי יִשְׂרָאֵל וְאָמַרְתָּ אֲלֵהֶם כִּי תָבֹאוּ אֶל הָאָרֶץ אֲשֶׁר אֲנִי נֹתֵן לָכֶם וּקְצַרְתֶּם אֶת קְצִירָהּ וַהֲבֵאתֶם אֶת עֹמֶר רֵאשִׁית קְצִירְכֶם אֶל הַכֹּהֵן:

Speak to the children of Israel and say to them: When you come to the Land which I am giving you, and you reap its harvest, you shall bring to the priest an Omer *from the beginning of your reaping.*

First Goes to G-d

TEXT 2

Rabbi Moshe Alshich, Vayikra ad loc.

לפי שאין דבר מחולל ומרים לב האדם ומחטיאם, כשפע רוב טוב... והן כל זה יפעל, בלתי הביט אל אלקים אשר נתנו. כי ישכחו ויאמרו: כוחם ועוצם ידם עשה להם את החייל ההוא.

על כן, אבינו שבשמים...אהבנו ומלמדנו מוסר השכל, כי מעת החל חרמש בקמת השעורים, שהיא ראשית כל תבואת הארץ, טרם רום לבבנו בראותנו רוב תבואות בבית ובשדה, בא הא-להים ללמדם דעת, כי לה' הארץ ומלואה... כי כח האדם אַיִן, כי הכל הבל.

There is nothing that makes a man cocky and arrogant and causes him to sin more than having abundant good fortune… All this causes one to not look towards the G-d who provided the bounty. They forget and claim that their own might and power brought them their success.

Therefore our Father in Heaven… loves us and teaches us the proper outlook. As soon as the scythe falls on the stalks of barley, the first of all grains, before our hearts swell at the sight of the bounty in the home and in the field, G-d comes to teach us: "The earth, and everything therein, belongs to G-d… man's power is nothingness, for everything is nothingness."

Rabbi Moshe Alshich
1508–1593

Born in Turkey; died and buried in Safed; student of the famed Rabbi Yosef Caro, the preeminent codifier of Jewish law. His biblical, homiletical, and ethical teachings remain popular to this day, including *Torat Moshe*, a commentary on the Torah. His students included Rabbi Chaim Vital and Rabbi Yom Tov Tsahalon.

Counting the Omer

TEXT 3

Vayikra 23:15-16

וּסְפַרְתֶּם לָכֶם מִמָּחֳרַת הַשַּׁבָּת מִיּוֹם הֲבִיאֲכֶם אֶת עֹמֶר הַתְּנוּפָה שֶׁבַע שַׁבָּתוֹת תְּמִימֹת תִּהְיֶינָה:

עַד מִמָּחֳרַת הַשַּׁבָּת הַשְּׁבִיעִת תִּסְפְּרוּ חֲמִשִּׁים יוֹם וְהִקְרַבְתֶּם מִנְחָה חֲדָשָׁה לַה':

And you shall count for yourselves, from the morrow of the rest day from the day you bring the Omer as a wave offering, seven weeks; they shall be complete.

Until the day following the seventh week shall you count [up to] fifty days, [on which] you shall bring a new meal offering to G-d.

TEXT 4

Rabbi Shneur Zalman of Liadi
(Alter Rebbe)
1745–1812

Chasidic rebbe, halachic authority, and founder of the Chabad movement. The Alter Rebbe was born in Liozna, Belarus, and was among the principal students of the Magid of Mezeritch. His numerous works include the *Tanya*, an early classic containing the fundamentals of Chabad Chasidism, and *Shulchan Aruch HaRav*, a code of Jewish law.

Shluchan Aruch Harav, Orach Chaim 489:1

מצות עשה מן התורה שיספור כל אחד מישראל שבעה שבועות ימים מיום הבאת קרבן העומר... ודרשו חכמים תספר לך, יכול בבית דין כמו ביובל שסופרין בבית דין שבע שבתות שנים ומקדשין שנת החמשים ליובל? תלמוד לומר: וספרתם לכם, כדי לסופרה לכל אחד ואחד ואין הציבור או שליח צבור יכולים לספור בעד כולם.

I t is a biblical mitzvah that every Jew should count seven weeks of days, beginning from when the Omer sacrifice is offered... The Sages expounded upon the words "Count for yourself." It might be thought that it is the Rabbinic court who conducts this count, in the same way that the Rabbinic court counts the seven 7-year cycles and then sanctifies the 50th year as the Jubilee year. But "Count for yourself" teaches us that each and every person must do the count. The congregational representatives are unable to count on behalf of the public.

Question—Days and Weeks

TEXT 5A

Siddur Nusach HaArizal, Liturgy of the Omer Count

הַיּוֹם שְׁמוֹנָה יָמִים שֶׁהֵם שָׁבוּעַ אֶחָד וְיוֹם אֶחָד לָעוֹמֶר .

Today is eight days, which is one week and one day to the Omer.

TEXT 5B

Shulchan Aruch Harav Ibid.

מן התורה צריך למנות הימים וגם השבועות, שנאמר תספרו חמשים יום, כלומר עד חמשים, ואומר שבעה שבועות תספר לך. כיצד יספור שניהם? כשמגיע לשבעה ימים יאמר היום שבעה ימים שהם שבוע אחד וכשמגיע ליום ארבעה עשר יאמר היום ארבעה עשר יום שהם שני שבועות ... ואם לא עשה כן, לא יצא ידי חובתו מן התורה.

The Torah instructs us to count both the number of days and the number of weeks, for it says, "Count fifty days," meaning, up until the 50th day, and it says "You shall count for yourself seven weeks." How does one count both? When he reaches the seventh day, he should say, "Today is the seventh day, which is one week." When he reaches the 14th day, he should say "Today is the 14th day, which is *two weeks."… If he does not do it in this manner, he has not fulfilled his biblical obligation.*

Question—All or Nothing

TEXT 6A

Rabbi Yaakov Ben Asher
(Tur, Baal Haturim)
ca. 1269–1343

Halachic authority and
codifier. Rabbi Ya'akov was
born in Germany and moved to
Toledo, Spain, with his father,
the noted halachist Rabbeinu
Asher, to escape persecution.
He wrote *Arba'ah Turim*,
an ingeniously organized
and highly influential
code of Jewish law. He is
considered one of the greatest
authorities of Halachah.

Rabbi Yaakov Baal Haturim, Tur Orach Chaim ch. 489

כתב בעל הלכות גדולות שאם שכח לברך באחד מן הימים, שלא יברך
עוד בימים שלאחריו. ורב סעדיה [גאון] כתב שאם שכח באחד מן
הימים, יברך בימים שלאחריו חוץ מלילה הראשון, שאם שכח ולא בירך
בו, שלא יברך עוד. ורב האי [גאון] כתב, בין בלילה הראשון ובין בשאר
לילות, אם שכח ולא בירך בו—יברך בשאר לילות.

The Baal Halachot Gedolot (Bahag) writes that if one forgot to make the blessing and count one of the days, he is not to make a blessing on any of the days that follow. Rav Saadiah Gaon writes that if one forgot to count a day, he does continue to make a blessing for the days that follow (except if he forgot to count the first night, in which case he does not make a blessing any further). Rav Hai Gaon writes that no matter when someone forgets to make a blessing, he may continue to make a blessing on the nights that follow.

TEXT 6B

Shulchan Aruch Harav 489:24

ולענין הלכה, נוהגין לספור בשאר לילות בלא ברכה, בין ששכח בלילה הראשון בין ששכח באחד משאר כל הלילות, לפי שספק ברכות להקל [ולדעת בעל הלכות גדולות, הברכה שלו היא לבטלה].

I n the final analysis: [If one forgot to count one of the nights] the custom is to count the rest of the nights without making a blessing, whether it was the first night that he forgot to count or any of the other nights. This is because of the rule, "Whenever there is doubt whether a blessing is to be made, we are lenient" (and according to the Bahag, such a blessing would be unjustified).

2. The Mystery of the *Sefirot*

Agricultural Roots

TEXT 7

Babylonian Talmud

A literary work of monumental proportions that draws upon the legal, spiritual, intellectual, ethical, and historical traditions of Judaism. The 37 tractates of the Babylonian Talmud contain the teachings of the Jewish sages from the period after the destruction of the 2nd Temple through the 5th century CE. It has served as the primary vehicle for the transmission of the Oral Law and the education of Jews over the centuries; it is the entry point for all subsequent legal, ethical, and theological Jewish scholarship.

Talmud Tractate Rosh Hashanah 16a

אמר רבי יהודה משום רבי עקיבא: מפני מה אמרה תורה הביאו עומר בפסח? מפני שהפסח זמן תבואה הוא. אמר הקדוש ברוך הוא: הביאו לפני עומר בפסח כדי שתתברך לכם תבואה שבשדות.

ומפני מה אמרה תורה הביאו בעצרת שתי הלחם בעצרת? מפני שעצרת זמן פירות האילן הוא, אמר הקדוש ברוך הוא: הביאו לפני שתי הלחם בעצרת כדי שיתברכו לכם פירות האילן.

Rabbi Yehudah said in the name of Rabbi Akiva: Why did the Torah tell us to bring the Omer *offering on Passover? Because Passover is the time of produce. G-d says, "Bring an* Omer *to Me on Passover so that I will bless for you the produce in the fields."*

And why did the Torah tell us to bring the shtei halechem *on Shavuot? Because Shavuot is the time of the fruits of the tree. G-d says, "Bring the* shtei halechem *to Me on Shavuot so that I will bless for you the fruits of the tree."*

TEXT 8

Rabbi Dovid ben Yoseph Abudraham
14th century

Resided in Seville, Spain, and is famous for his work on Jewish prayers and blessings. The work—completed around the year 1340—is a commentary on the daily, Shabbat, and festival prayers and collects many customs and laws relating to them. He is believed to have been a disciple of Rabbi Yaakov ben Asher, author of *Arba'ah Turim*.

Rabbi Dovid Abudraham, Abudraham, Order of the Prayers for Passover

מפני שהעולם בצער מפסח עד שבועות על התבואות ועל האילנות שיצליחו, כדאיתא בפרק קמא דראש השנה: תניא אמר רבי יהודה מפני מה אמרה תורה הביאו עומר בפסח, מפני שהפסח זמן תבואה הוא ... כדי שתתברך לכם תבואה שבשדות ...

לפיכך ציווה הקדוש ברוך הוא לספור ימים אלו כדי שנזכור צער העולם ולשוב אליו בלבב שלם ולהתחנן לפניו לרחם עלינו ועל הבריות ועל הארץ שיהיו התבואות כתיקונן שהם סיבת חיינו, שאם אין קמח אין תורה.

rom Passover until Shavuot, the world is anxious about the success of the produce and the orchards. As it is stated in the first chapter of tractate Rosh Hashanah: "Why did the Torah tell us to bring the Omer offering on Passover? Because Passover is the time of produce… so that I will bless for you the produce in the fields."

G-d therefore commanded us to count these days, in order to highlight the world's anxiety [and thus be inspired] to return to him with complete hearts and to supplicate before Him to have mercy upon us, upon the creatures and upon the land—that the grain crops, which sustain our lives, be proper, for "if there is no flour, there is no Torah."

The Kabbalistic Element

TEXT 9

Siddur Nusach HaArizal ibid.

רִבּוֹנוֹ שֶׁל עוֹלָם, אַתָּה צִוִּיתָנוּ עַל יְדֵי מֹשֶׁה עַבְדֶּךָ לִסְפּוֹר סְפִירַת
הָעוֹמֶר כְּדֵי לְטַהֲרֵנוּ מִקְּלִפּוֹתֵינוּ וּמִטֻּמְאוֹתֵינוּ... וּבְכֵן יְהִי רָצוֹן מִלְּפָנֶיךָ ה'
אֱלֹקֵינוּ וֵאלֹקֵי אֲבוֹתֵינוּ, שֶׁבִּזְכוּת סְפִירַת הָעוֹמֶר שֶׁסָּפַרְתִּי הַיּוֹם, יְתֻקַּן
מַה שֶּׁפָּגַמְתִּי בִּסְפִירָה [פלונית השייך לאותו הלילה] וְאֶטָּהֵר וְאֶתְקַדֵּשׁ
בִּקְדֻשָּׁה שֶׁל מַעְלָה, וְעַל יְדֵי זֶה יֻשְׁפַּע שֶׁפַע רַב בְּכָל הָעוֹלָמוֹת וּלְתַקֵּן
אֶת נַפְשׁוֹתֵינוּ וְרוּחוֹתֵינוּ וְנִשְׁמוֹתֵינוּ מִכָּל סִיג וּפְגַם, וּלְטַהֲרֵנוּ וּלְקַדְּשֵׁנוּ
בִּקְדֻשָּׁתְךָ הָעֶלְיוֹנָה, אָמֵן סֶלָה.

Master of the universe, You have commanded us through Moses Your servant to count Sefirat Haomer, *in order to purify us from our evil and uncleanness. As You have written in Your Torah,* "You shall count for yourselves from the day following the day of rest, from the day on which you bring the Omer as a wave-offering; [the counting] shall be for seven full weeks. Until the day following the seventh week shall you count [up to] fifty days," *so that the souls of Your people Israel may be cleansed from their defilement.*

Therefore, may it be Your will, Lord our G-d and G-d of our fathers, that in the merit of the Sefirat Haomer which I counted today, the blemish that I have caused in the Sefirah [Sefirah of that day] be rectified, and that I may be purified and sanctified with supernal holiness. May abundant bounty thereby be bestowed upon all the worlds. May it rectify our nefesh, ruach, *and* neshamah *from every baseness and defect, and may it purify and sanctify us with Your supernal holiness. Amen, selah.*

3. Preparing for the Big Day

Eager Anticipation

TEXT 10

Midrash

למה מונין ספירה מפסח ועד עצרת יותר מבשאר מועדים? משל למה הדבר דומה למלך אחד שרכב בדרך ומצא אדם אחד מושלך בבור שהיה אסור שם, אמר לו המלך אני אעלה אותך ואוציא אותך מבור הזה ולזמן פלוני אתן לך את בתי. ושמח אותו האדם שמחה גדולה, אמר לא די שמוציאני מבור זה אלא עוד רוצה ליתן לי בתו. וכן עשה המלך, הוציאו מהבור והלבישו בגדים נאים וכסף וזהב נתן לו. כשראה אותו האיש כך שהמלך קיים כבר מקצת דבריו התחיל למנות מיד כמה זמן יש למה שקבע המלך לתת לו בתו... כך היו ישראל במצרים כמו בבור וכו'.

Why do we count the days between Passover and Shavuot, more so than any other festivals?

This can be compared to a king who was out riding and found a man who had been cast into a pit. The king told him, "I will pull you out of this pit, and on this-and-this day, I will give you my daughter as a wife." The man grew tremendously happy and said to himself, "Not only will he take me out of this pit, but he also wants to give me his daughter!" And the king did just that. He took the man out of the pit, dressed him in fine clothes, and gave him gold and silver.

When the man saw that the king was true to his word, he began to count to the date when the king had pledged he would give him his daughter…

The Jews in Egypt were as if in a pit…

Preparing the Character

TEXT 11

Zohar Chadash, Yitro §6

וכיון ש[אישה] יצאה [מטומאתה], משם ולהלאה "וספרה לה" (שבעת ימים), אף כאן ישראל, כשיצאו ממצרים יצאו מן הטומאה ועשו פסח לאכול על שלחן אביהם … משם ולהלאה יעשו חשבון לקרב אשה לבעלה, שתתחבר עמו, ואלו הם חמשים ימים של טהרה לבוא לסוד עולם הבא … ולקבל התורה ולקרב אשה לבעלה.

When a woman leaves her impurity, she begins "to count for herself" (seven days). So too, when the Jewish people left Egypt, they left their impurity and made the Passover sacrifice to eat on their table of their Father. From that point, they started to count towards bringing together the woman to her husband to unite with him. These are the 50 days of purity needed to reach the secret of

Zohar
The seminal work of Kabbalah, Jewish mysticism. The Zohar is a mystical commentary on the Torah, written in Aramaic and Hebrew. According to Arizal, the Zohar contains the teachings of Rabbi Shimon bar Yocha'i who lived in the Land of Israel during the 2nd century. The Zohar has become one of the indispensable texts of traditional Judaism, alongside and nearly equal in stature to the Mishnah and Talmud.

the World to Come ... and to receive the Torah and bring a wife close to her husband.

49-Step Program

TEXT 12A

Rabbi Menachem Mendel Schneerson
1902–1994

The towering Jewish leader of the 20th century, known as "the Lubavitcher Rebbe," or simply as "the Rebbe." Born in southern Ukraine, the Rebbe escaped Nazi occupied Europe, arriving in the U.S. in June 1941. The Rebbe inspired and guided the revival of traditional Judaism after the European devastation, impacting virtually every Jewish community the world over. The Rebbe often emphasized that the performance of just one additional good deed could usher in the era of Mashiach. The Rebbe's scholarly talks and writings have been printed in more than 200 volumes.

The Lubavitcher Rebbe, Torat Menachem vol. 3 (5711) p. 65-67

ענין ספירת העומר... הוא בירור המדות עצמן, [ו]אין מספיק על זה הבירור בכללות אלא צריך להיות בירור פרטי, הבירור דכל מדה ומדה בפני עצמה, ועוד זאת, גם הבירור בכל מדה כפי שהיא כלולה משאר המדות....

ויובן זה על דרך משל ממידת החסד, שהיא כלולה מכל המידות. דענין מידת החסד עצמה היא אהבת ה', וחסד שבחסד הוא מה שאוהב את אוהבי ה', שיש לו אהבה למי שעוסק בלימוד התורה וקיום המצוות ביראת שמים, ועוד זאת, שמצד אהבת ה' הרי הוא זריז בקיום המצוות שלו.

וענין גבורה שבחסד הוא מה שמצד אהבתו לה' הרי הוא שונא את מנגדי ה'.

וענין תפארת שבחסד הוא כאשר מתפאר ומתייפה מהחסד, דכשרואה כיצד אדם לומד תורה בהתלהבות ומקיים מצוות בהתלהבות, הרי הוא מתפאר על היופי שבתורה ומצוות עד היכן יכולה התורה לפעול באדם. נצח שבחסד הוא כאשר מצד אהבתו לה', הרי כשישנם מונעים ומעכבים, הרי הוא לוחם עם המנגדים.

ועוד זאת, דכאשר יש התנגדות מבחוץ ואין לו כח להתגבר אליהם... הרי מצד אהבתו את ה', הוא מנצח את עצמו להסיר את המניעות והעיכובים – וזהו ענין הוד שבחסד.

ועניין יסוד שבחסד הוא, דגם כאשר מאיזה טעם אין לו משיכה לתורה ומצות, הרי מצד אהבתו לה', הוא מתקשר לזה בכל נפשו עד שמתעורר בתשוקה לתורה ומצות.

ועניין מלכות שבחסד הוא, מה שכל המחשבה, דיבור ומעשה שלו הם רק בתורה ומצות מצד אהבה זו.

והנה את זה לעומת זה עשה האלקים... וכך בנפש הבהמית כל מדה משבע המדות, כלולה מכל המדות. וכמו במדת החסד על דרך משל: עניין חסד שבחסד הוא מה שאהבתו לדברים גשמיים באה לידי ביטוי בתשוקה גלויה לגשמיות.

וגבורה שבחסד היא מה שמצד אהבתו ותשוקתו לדברים גשמיים הוא שונא את המנגד לזה, דהאומרים לו איך מתאים לך להיות שקוע בעניינים בהמיים שאינם לפי מעלת האדם—הרי הוא שונא אותם.

ותפארת שבחסד הוא מה שנוסף לזה שהוא נמשך לעניינים גשמיים, הנה עוד זאת שהוא מתפאר בה ומתגאה בזה ומתלהב מזה.

נצח שבחסד הוא, שגם כאשר מאיזו סיבה חסרה אצלו המשיכה לדברים גשמיים, הרי הוא מנצח את עצמו ופועל תשוקה בעצמו.

ועוד יותר, דגם כשיש לו מנגדים מבחוץ המביישים ומבזים אותו ואומרים ראו כיצד יהודי בן אברהם יצחק ויעקב שקוע בעניינים בהמיים, ועוד יותר בעניינים אסורים, הרי הוא לוחם שזה לא יבלבל את תאוותו—שהו עניין הוד שבחסד.

ועניין יסוד שבחסד הוא ההתקשרות בהתאוה.

עד שגם המחשבה, דיבור ומעשה שלו הם בעניינים חומריים... שזהו עניין מלכות שבחסד שבנפש.

The idea of Sefirat Haomer *is to perfect our* middot [=sefirot]. *To do this, it is not enough to refine ourselves broadly, but there must be a detailed refinement, one middah at a time. Furthermore,* *each individual* middah *must undergo a detailed refinement, perfecting each sub-*middah *component.*

Take, for example, Chesed. Chesed *itself is comprised of all seven* middot. Chesed *in and of itself is love [in this instance love] of G-d.* Chesed Sh'beChesed *is to love those who love G-d; he loves those who study Torah and fulfill the* mitzvot *with fear of Heaven. Additionally, his love of G-d drives him to fulfill the* mitzvot *assiduously.*

Gevurah Sh'beChesed *is that, because of his love of G-d, he despises those who oppose Him.*

Tiferet Sh'beChesed *is that he finds glory and beautification in his* Chesed. *For example, when he sees someone studying Torah and fulfilling* mitzvot *with enthusiasm, he soars with the beauty of Torah and* mitzvot, *struck by how much Torah is able to affect a person.*

Netzach Sh'beChesed *is that, because of his love of G-d, he goes into unrelenting battle against all obstacles that prevent his divine service.*

Hod Sh'beChesed *is that even when he cannot vanquish those forces which oppose G-d, he still resolves to remain unaffected by them.*

Yesod Sh'beChesed *is that even when he has no particular attraction to Torah and* mitzvot, *his love of*

G-d drives him to apply himself to them completely, causing such an attraction to develop.

Malchut Sh'beChesed *is that each and every one of his deeds—what he thinks, what he says, and the way he acts—is all devoted to Torah and* mitzvot, *because of this love.*

However, G-d made everything with a counterpart. Thus, the animal soul also has these seven traits, each comprised of all seven middot. *To use the example of Chesed:* Chesed Sh'beChesed *[of the animal soul] is that his love for material things expresses itself in an overt passion for materialism.* Gevurah Sh'beChesed *is that his love for material things causes him to hate those who opposed such conduct. He despises those who tell him, "How is it fitting for you to be mired in these animalistic matters which are not becoming of a human being?"*

Tiferet Sh'beChesed *is that not only is he attracted to material matters, but he is excited by them and is proud and vainglorious about them.*

Netzach Sh'beChesed *is that even when his attraction to materialism is deficient, he prevails over himself and forces such a desire.*

Hod Sh'beChesed *is that even when there are those who mock him by saying, "Look at this Jew, a descendant of the Patriarchs [and thus capable of living* a holy life], *who is mired in those animalistic things, even in forbidden things,*" he makes sure that their mocking does not affect his desire.

Yesod Sh'beChesed *is to forge a bond with the animalistic passion.*

Malchut Sh'beChesed *is that thoughts, words, and deeds all revolve around these coarse things.*

Two Answers

TEXT 12B

Ibid. p. 65

וזהו מה שבספירת העומר יש שני ענינים: מצוה למימני יומי ומצוה למימני שבועי. דענין למימני שבועי קאי על בירור כל מדה בכללות וענין מצוה למימני יומי קאי על בירור כל פרט שבכל מידה.

This is *why* Sefirat Haomer *has two parts to it. There is a mitzvah to count the days, and a mitzvah to count the weeks. The weekly count represents the refinement of each trait as a whole, and the daily count represents the refinement of each middah in detail.*

Conclusion—Every Day Counts

TEXT 13

Rabbi Yisrael Baal Shem Tov, Tzava'at Harivash §17

לא להניח שום יום בלא מצוה, הן מצוה קלה או חמורה... והוא דבר
גדול מאוד כי אז ידע שעשה פעולה ביום זה, שברא מלאך אחד ואם
יש [עליו] מלאך מליץ אחד וגו'.

No day should be left without a mitzvah, whether it be a minor mitzvah or a major one... This is of great importance; for then one will always know that he achieved something that day; that he created one angel, and that one angel is now interceding on his behalf.

Rabbi Yisrael Baal Shem Tov (Besht) 1698–1760

Founder of the Chasidic movement. Born in Slutsk, Belarus, the Baal Shem Tov was orphaned as a child. He served as a teacher's assistant and clay digger before founding the Chasidic movement and revolutionizing the Jewish world with his emphasis on prayer, joy, and love for every Jew, regardless of his or her level of Torah knowledge.

TEXT 14

The Lubavitcher Rebbe, Hayom Yom Entry for 1 Iyar

פעם אמרו לאדמו"ר הרש"ב: חסידי אדמו"ר הזקן היו תמיד סופרים. הפתגם מצא חן בעיניו ואמר: זוהי ענינה של עבודה. השעות צריכות להיות ספורות ואז גם הימים ספורים. כשיום הולך יש לדעת מה פעלו ומה יש לפעול בעתיד. בכלל, יש להשתדל שהמחר יהיה יותר יפה מאתמול.

It was once related to the Rebbe Rashab: "The Alter Rebbe's chassidim were always keeping count." My father took a great liking to the saying, and he commented: "That idea characterizes man's avodah. The hours must be 'counted hours,' then the days will be 'counted days.' When a day passes one should know what he has accomplished and what remains yet to be done... In general, one should always see to it that tomorrow should be much better than today."

5

BEHAR-BECHUKOTAI

Cash Up Front

Lessons from Contract Law

Student Manual

PARSHA OVERVIEW
Behar-Bechukotai

On the mountain of Sinai, G-d communicates to Moses the laws of the Sabbatical year: every seventh year, all work on the land should cease, and its produce becomes free for the taking for all, man and beast.

Seven Sabbatical cycles are followed by a fiftieth year—the Jubilee year, on which work on the land ceases, all indentured servants are set free, and all ancestral estates in the Holy Land that have been sold revert to their original owners.

Behar also contains additional laws governing the sale of lands, and the prohibitions against fraud and usury.

G-d promises that if the people of Israel will keep His commandments, they will enjoy material prosperity and dwell secure in their homeland. But He also delivers a harsh "rebuke," warning of the exile, persecution and other evils that will befall them if they abandon their covenant with Him.

Nevertheless, "Even when they are in the land of their enemies, I will not cast them away; nor will I ever abhor them, to destroy them and to break My covenant with them; for I am the L-rd their G-d."

The Parshah concludes with the rules on how to calculate the values of different types of pledges made to G-d, and the mitzvah of tithing produce and livestock.

1. Buying and Selling

The Laws of Acquisition

TEXT 1

Vayikra 25:14

וְכִי תִמְכְּרוּ מִמְכָּר לַעֲמִיתֶךָ אוֹ קָנֹה מִיַּד עֲמִיתֶךָ אַל תּוֹנוּ אִישׁ אֶת אָחִיו:

And when you make a sale to your fellow Jew or make an acquisition from the hand of your fellow Jew, you shall not wrong one another.

TEXT 2A

Talmud Tractate Bava Metzia 47b

אמר רבי יוחנן: דבר תורה מעות קונות, ומפני מה אמרו משיכה קונה? גזירה שמא יאמר לו נשרפו חטיך בעלייה.

סוף סוף, מאן דשדא דליקה בעי שלומי!

אלא, גזירה שמא תפול דליקה באונס. אי מוקמת להו ברשותיה מסר נפשיה, טרח ומציל, ואי לא, לא מסר נפשיה טרח ומציל.

ריש לקיש אמר: משיכה מפורשת מן התורה.

מאי טעמא דריש לקיש? אמר קרא, "וכי תמכרו ממכר לעמיתך או קנה מיד עמיתך"—דבר הנקנה מיד ליד.

Rabbi Yochanan said: By Biblical law, [the delivery of] money affects possession. Why then was it said meshichah [pulling the item] affects possession? Lest the vendor say to the buyer, "Your wheat was burnt in the loft."

But after all, whoever causes the fire must make compensation!

But [for fear] lest a fire accidentally break out. Now, if the ownership is still vested in the vendor, he will wholeheartedly take pains to save it; if not, he will not do so.

Babylonian Talmud
A literary work of monumental proportions that draws upon the legal, spiritual, intellectual, ethical, and historical traditions of Judaism. The 37 tractates of the Babylonian Talmud contain the teachings of the Jewish sages from the period after the destruction of the 2nd Temple through the 5th century CE. It has served as the primary vehicle for the transmission of the Oral Law and the education of Jews over the centuries; it is the entry point for all subsequent legal, ethical, and theological Jewish scholarship.

TEXT 2B

Rashi, Tractate Bava Metzai 46b

"[סבר לה] כרבי יוחנן". דאמר לקמן "דבר תורה מעות קונות", כדאשכחן גבי קונה מן ההקדש, שאמרה תורה "ונתן הכסף וקם לו".

"As Rabbi Yochanan" states, "Biblically, money effects acquisition," for we find that regarding acquiring something from sacred property, Scripture uses the term, "And he gives the money... and it shall be his."

Rabbi Shlomo Yitschaki
(Rashi)
1040–1105
Most noted biblical and Talmudic commentator. Born in Troyes, France, Rashi studied in the famed *yeshivot* of Mainz and Worms. His commentaries on the Pentateuch and the Talmud, which focus on the straightforward meaning of the text, have appeared in virtually every edition of the Talmud and Bible.

Rabbi Yochanan Rules

TEXT 3A

Rabbi Moshe ben Maimon
(Maimonides, Rambam)
1135–1204
Halachist, philosopher, author, and physician. Maimonides was born in Cordoba, Spain. After the conquest of Cordoba by the Almohads, he fled Spain and eventually settled in Cairo, Egypt. There, he became the leader of the Jewish community and served as court physician to the vizier of Egypt. He is most noted for authoring the *Mishneh Torah*, an encyclopedic arrangement of Jewish law, and for his philosophical work, *Guide for the Perplexed*.

Maimonides, Mishneh Torah Laws of Sale 3:1

אחד הבהמה ואחד שאר המטלטלין נקנין במעות דין תורה, ומשנתן את המעות קנה ואין אחד מהן יוכל לחזור בו, אבל חכמים תקנו שלא יקנו המטלטלין אלא בהגבהה או במשיכת דבר שאין דרכו להגביה.

According to Scriptural law, both livestock and other movable property are acquired by the payment of money. Once the purchaser pays the money, neither he nor the seller can retract [unilaterally]. The Sages, however, enacted that movable property should be acquired only through lifting up the article (hagbahah) or pulling (meshichah) an article that is not commonly lifted up.

TEXT 3B

Ibid. 3:5-6

למה תקנו חכמים דבר זה במטלטלין?

גזרה שמא יתן הלוקח דמי החפץ וקודם שיקחנו יאבד באונס, וכגון שנפלה דליקה ונשרף, או באו ליסטים ונטלוהו, אם יהיה ברשות הלוקח יתמהמה המוכר ולא יצילהו, לפיכך העמידוהו חכמים ברשות המוכר כדי שישתדל ויציל החפץ, שאם אבד חייב לשלם.

נמצאת אומר שאם נתן דמי המקח ונאנס קודם שיקחנו, ואמר לו הלוקח תן לי מקחי או החזר לי את מעותי, ואף על פי שיש עדים

שאבד באונס ולא היה במוכר כח להצילו ולא נתרשל בדבר, הרי זה מחזיר את הדמים, שהרי תקנו חכמים משיכה.

לפיכך אם היה ביתו של לוקח שיש בו החפץ שנמכר מושכר למוכר, לא תקנו לו חכמים משיכה, שהרי המקח ברשות הלוקח, ומשנתן את הדמים נקנה המקח ואין אחד מהן יכול לחזור בו.

W hy did our Sages make such an ordinance with regard to movable property?

This decree was enacted lest a purchaser pay for an article and, before he takes possession of it, it be destroyed by factors beyond his control—e.g., a fire breaks out and burns it, or thieves come and take it. If the article is considered as in the possession of the purchaser, the seller may hesitate and not endeavor to save it.

For this reason, our Sages ordained that the article remains the possession of the seller, so that he will endeavor to save it for, if it is destroyed, he is obligated to pay [to return the original funds].

Thus, if a purchaser paid for an article and it was destroyed by forces beyond his control before he took it, the purchaser may tell the seller, "Give me the article I purchased or return my money." Even though there are witnesses who saw that the article was destroyed by forces beyond his control, [i.e.,] the seller could not save it, and he was not lazy regarding the matter, the seller must return the money. For our Sages ordained that a kinyan is finalized through meshichah *[and therefore the onus is on the seller to provide the purchaser with the article].*

For this reason, if the purchaser owned the house in which the sold article was held, and he was renting it to the seller, our Sages did not ordain that the article must be acquired through meshichah. *For the article that was sold is in the domain of the purchaser. In this instance, once he pays the money, the sale is concluded, and neither can retract.*

Not Backing Out

TEXT 4

Maimonides Ibid. 7:1-2

מי שנתן הדמים ולא משך הפירות, אף על פי שלא נקנו המטלטלין כמו שביארנו, כל החוזר בו בין לוקח בין מוכר לא עשה מעשה ישראל וחייב לקבל מי שפרע ואפילו נתן הערבון כל החוזר מקבל מי שפרע. וכיצד מקבל מי שפרע, אוררין אותו בבית דין ואומרין מי שפרע מאנשי דור המבול ומאנשי דור הפלגה ומאנשי סדום ועמורה וממצרים שטבעו בים הוא יפרע ממי שאינו עומד בדבורו, ואחר כך יחזור הדמים.

hen one pays the money, but does not perform meshichah *on the produce, although the purchaser does not acquire the movable property, as we have explained, whoever retracts—whether the purchaser or the seller—is considered to have conducted himself in a shameful manner.*

He is liable to receive [the admonishment of] "mi shepara." Even if the purchaser only made a deposit, if either of the parties involved retracts, that party is eligible to receive [the admonishment of] mi shepara.

What does receiving [the admonishment of] mi shepara involve? He is cursed in the court and told: "May He who exacted retribution from the generation of the flood, the generation of the dispersal, the inhabitants of Sodom and Gomorrah, and the Egyptians who drowned in the sea exact retribution from one who does not keep his word."

After this curse is administered, the seller should return the money.

Optional Section
Verbal Agreements

TEXT 5A

Shulchan Aruch Choshen Mishpat 204:7

הנושא ונותן בדברים בלבד, הרי זה ראוי לו לעמוד בדבורו אף על פי שלא לקח מהדמים כלום, ולא רשם ולא הניח משכון. וכל החוזר בו, בין לוקח בין מוכר, אף על פי שאינו חייב לקבל מי שפרע הרי זה ממחוסרי אמנה ואין רוח חכמים נוחה הימנו.

Rabbi Yosef Caro
(Maran, *Beit Yosef*)
1488–1575

Halachic authority and author. Rabbi Caro was born in Spain, but was forced to flee during the expulsion in 1492 and eventually settled in Safed, Israel. He authored many works including the *Beit Yosef*, *Kesef Mishneh*, and a mystical work, *Magid Meisharim*. Rabbi Caro's magnum opus, the Shulchan Aruch (Code of Jewish Law), has been universally accepted as the basis for modern Jewish law.

When one performs a business transaction based only on verbal agreement—without any deposit or other record—it is appropriate that he honor the deal even if money has not yet changed hands, no notation has been made, and no collateral given. Anyone who reneges on a verbal commitment—whether the buyer or the seller—though he is not liable for mi shepara, has acted dishonestly and the Sages were displeased with such behavior.

TEXT 5B

Rabbi Moshe Isserles, Glosses of Rama to Shulchan Aruch Ibid 204:11.

אין רוח חכמים נוחה הימנו. והני מילי בחד תרעא, אבל בתרי תרעי אין זה ממחוסרי אמנה....
ויש אומרים דאפילו בתרי תרעי אסור לחזור, ואם חזר בו יש בו משום מחוסר אמנה. וכן נראה עיקר.

The Sages were not pleased with such behavior. However, in the event that the market prices fluctuated, it is not considered dishonest…

Some argue and say that even in a situation of fluctuating prices, one is forbidden to renege, and if he does, it is considered dishonest.

The latter opinion appears authoritative.

Rabbi Moshe Isserles (Rema)
1525–1572

Halachist. Rama served as rabbi in Krakow, Poland, and is considered the definitive authority on Jewish law among Ashkenazic Jewry. Rama authored glosses on the Shulchan Aruch (known as the *Mapah*) and *Darchei Moshe*, a commentary on the halachic compendium *Arba'ah Turim*.

TEXT 5C

Rabbi Yechiel Michel Epstein, Aruch Hashulchan Choshen Mishpat ibid.

ונראה דמדינא וודאי אין בזה משום מחוסרי אמנה רק ממידת חסידות.

From a strictly legal perspective, it is not considered dishonest [to renege on a verbal agreement when the values have changed]; rather, it falls under the category of pious conduct.

Rabbi Yechiel Michel Halevi Epstein
1829–1908

Noted author of Jewish law. Rabbi Epstein lived in Czarist Lithuania and was chief rabbi of Novozypkov, a town near Minsk, and later, of Navahrudak, where he served until his death. A prolific writer, his primary work is *Aruch Hashulchan*, an expanded and reworked code of Jewish law.

TEXT 6A

Talmud Tractate Makot 24a

"ודובר אמת בלבבו". כגון רב ספרא.

"Speaks truth in his heart," such as Rabbi Safra.

TEXT 6B

Rashi ad loc.

"רב ספרא", בשאלתות דרב אחא. והכי הוה עובדא דרב ספרא: היה לו
חפץ אחד למכור ובא אדם אחד לפניו בשעה שהיה קורא קריאת שמע
ואמר לו תן לי החפץ בכך וכך דמים ולא ענהו מפני שהיה קורא קריאת
שמע כסבור זה שלא היה רוצה ליתנו בדמים הללו והוסיף אמר תנהו
לי בכך יותר לאחר שסיים קריאת שמע אמר לו טול החפץ בדמים
שאמרת בראשונה שבאותן דמים היה דעתי ליתנם לך.

The story can be found in the She'iltot of Rabbi
Acha: Rabbi Safra had an item for sale and
a certain individual approached him while he
was reciting the Shema and said, "Give the item to me
for such-and-such a price." Rabbi Safra did not respond
as he was reciting the Shema [when interruptions are
forbidden] and the buyer figured that he didn't want
to settle for such a low price, so he said, "Sell it to me
for this higher sum."

After Rabbi Safra concluded reciting the Shema, he
said, "Please take the item for the original price you
quoted, for I originally intended to sell it to you for
that price."

2. Money Matters

A Lottery Question

TEXT 7A

*Rabbi Moshe Isserles, Glosses of Rama
to Shulchan Aruch Choshen Mishpat 198:5*

ויש אומרים דאם היו המטלטלין במקום דליכא למיחש לדליקה,
נקנו במעות.

Some state that if the movable object was in a place where there is no concern for casualty, money can complete the sale.

TEXT 7B

Rabbi Shabetai Cohen, Shach ad loc. §9

והבית יוסף כתב ריש סימן זה שאין נראה כן מדברי הפוסקים. וכן בדין,
דלא נתנו חכמים דבריהם לשיעורים... וכן נראה לי עיקר.

The Bet Yosef *writes in the beginning of this chapter that from the words of the* halachic *authorities, it does not appear to be so. And rightfully so, for the Rabbis did not give [such] limitations to their words… This appears to me as the decisive ruling.*

Rabbi Shabetai ben Meir Hakohen (Shach)
1621–1662

Also known by the acronym "Shach," after his definitive commentary on Jewish law, *Siftei Kohen*; he was a noted Lithuanian talmudist and authority on Jewish law. At a very young age, Rabbi Shabetai was appointed to the Vilna Rabbinical Court. *Siftei Kohen*, written when he was 24, is an essential legal commentary on *the Yoreh De'ah* and *Choshen Mishpat* sections of the Shulachan Aruch. When Polish Jewry was devastated by the Chmielnicki Uprisings, Rabbi Shabetai fled to Czechoslovakia.

Meat for the Festival

TEXT 8A

Shulchan Aruch Choshen Mishpat 199:3

יש זמן שמעות קונות, שהעמידו חכמים דבריהם על דין תורה בבשר
בארבעה פרקים, ואלו הם: ערב יום טוב האחרון של חג, וערב יום טוב
הראשון של פסח, וערב העצרת, וערב ראש השנה.

There are times money alone does complete the acquisition, for the Rabbis reverted to the Scriptural law regarding meat during four periods within the year: Before the festivals of Shemini Atzeret [Simchat Torah], Passover, Shavuot, and Rosh Hashanah.

TEXT 8B

Rama ad loc.

ויש מי שכתב דהוא הדין הנותן מעות על יין לקידוש בערב שבת, דקנה,
דכל כהאי גוונא העמידו דבריהם על דין תורה.

Some suggest that a similar law applies when one gives money to purchase wine for kiddush before Shabbat. In all such cases, the Rabbis deferred to Scriptural law.

TEXT 9

Rabbi Yisrael Meir Kagan, Mishneh Berurah,
Biur Halachah to Orach Chayim §656

כתב הפרי מגדים... דאם נתן מעות על יין לקידוש קונה דדין תורה
מעות קונה והעמידו על דבר תורה בקנית מצוה, אם כן יש לומר דהוא
הדין אתרוג ושניהם אין יכולין לחזור בו.

T he Peri Megadim *writes that just as money finalizes the acquisition with regards to purchasing wine for* kiddush—*for the Rabbis reverted to Scriptural law with regards to purchasing for a mitzvah—the same would apply to purchasing an etrog, and both parties are not allowed to renege [once money has transferred hands].*

Rabbi Yisrael Meir Hakohen Kagan
(*Chafets Chayim*)
1839–1933
Pre-WWII Polish Halachist and ethicist. Rabbi Kagan was the dean of the illustrious yeshivah in Radin, Poland. A prolific author on topics of Halachah and ethical behavior, he is often called *Chafets Chayim* after his first work, a comprehensive digest of laws pertaining to ethical speech. His magnum opus, on which he worked for 28 years, is *Mishnah Berurah*, a concise commentary on the first section of the Shulchan Aruch. He also authored *Bi'ur Halachah* on the Shulchan Aruch and numerous other works.

3. G-d's Purchase

The Soul of Acquisition

TEXT 10

Bereishit (Genesis) 14:19

וַיְבָרְכֵהוּ וַיֹּאמַר בָּרוּךְ אַבְרָם לְאֵ-ל עֶלְיוֹן קֹנֵה שָׁמַיִם וָאָרֶץ:

And he blessed him, and he said, "Blessed be Abram to the Most High G-d, who acquired heaven and earth."

TEXT 11

Rabbi Menachem Mendel Schneersohn of Lubavitch
(*Tzemech Tsedek*)
1789–1866
Chasidic Rebbe and noted author. The *Tzemech Tsedek* was the third leader of the Chabad Chasidic movement and a noted authority on Jewish law. His numerous works include halachic responsa, Chasidic discourses, and Kabbalistic writings. Active in the affairs of Russian Jewry, he worked to alleviate the plight of the Cantonists, Jewish children kidnapped to serve in the Czar's army. He passed away in Lubavitch, leaving seven sons and two daughters.

Rabbi Menachem Mendel Schneersohn of Lubavitch, the Tzemach Tzedek, Derech Mitzvotecha p. 36b-37a

ידוע דעצמותו יתברך רם ונשא רבבות מדריגות עד אין קץ מגדר ובחינת עלמין... כי אין ערוך ממש אליו יתברך אלא שבחינה זו הנקרא סובב הוא רק הארה ממנו ברוך הוא וכמו הזיו שאינו מערך עצמיות המאור... הנה באמת היא ירידה גדולה קמיה יתברך והשפלה שמשפיל עצמו יתברך במילין דהדיוטא להיות מקור לחיות העולמות.

G-d's essence is far loftier, myriads of levels loftier **ad infinitum**, than this world... for the worlds cannot relate to G-d. The level of G-d that does indeed relate to this world is a mere ray of His essence, incomparable to the luminescence of G-d Himself...

To lower Himself to relate with earthly matters and act as the origins of this world is indeed a great descent for G-d.

TEXT 12A

The Lubavitcher Rebbe, Sefer Hasichot 5749 vol. 2 p. 682

ענין ה"מכירה" בעבודת האדם לקונו ("לתקן הדעות"), הוא, עך דרך מה שכתוב "קונה שמים וארץ", "שה' יתברך קונה מהתחתונים ובפרט מישראל עם סגולתו", ש(מוכרים ו)מקנים לו כל עניני העולם, מוציאים אותם מהמעמד ומצב ד"רשות הרבים", טורי דפרודא, ומעלים אותם ל"רשות היחיד", יחידו של עולם.

The idea of a sale in man's Divine service is similar to what is stated, "G-d who acquires heaven and earth," namely, that G-d "acquires" the lower realms from His nation the Jews. The Jews effectively transfer ownership of this world to G-d by taking it out from a state of divisiveness and distance from G-d and elevating it to a singular domain, united with G-d.

Rabbi Menachem Mendel Schneerson
1902–1994

The towering Jewish leader of the 20th century, known as "the Lubavitcher Rebbe," or simply as "the Rebbe." Born in southern Ukraine, the Rebbe escaped Nazi occupied Europe, arriving in the U.S. in June 1941. The Rebbe inspired and guided the revival of traditional Judaism after the European devastation, impacting virtually every Jewish community the world over. The Rebbe often emphasized that the performance of just one additional good deed could usher in the era of Mashiach. The Rebbe's scholarly talks and writings have been printed in more than 200 volumes.

TEXT 13A

Derech Mitzvotecha ibid.

וזהו סוד המשיכה, שהוא יתברך מושך החפץ.

This is the secret of meshichah: G-d pulls the objects.

TEXT 13B

Ibid.

ואחר המשיכה הוא יתברך נותן כסף... ממשיך מלמעלה גלוי אור אין סוף ברוך הוא בכל העולמות ומשם מאיר הארה רבה ועצומה עד להפליא על נפשו... וממנה יבא אהבה רבה זו בנפש האדם אשר בגוף וזהו סוד הכסף מלשון כוסף ואהבה רבה.

After the act of meshichah, G-d gives the "money"... [namely,] the person draws down a G-dly revelation throughout all the worlds, and from there, a spectacular light shines in his soul... from which a fiery love is born in the soul within his body. This is the idea of kesef [money], a term denoting kosef, love.

We Trust Your Soul

TEXT 13C

Ibid 37b.

דעת רבי יוחנן שדבר תורה מעות קונות. והענין כי לפעמים נותנים
הסוחרים הכסף קודם המשיכה וכן יש למעלה גם כן המשכת מ"ד
לעורר מ"ן כידוע, שגם כדי שיהיה אתערותא דלתתא צריך להיות סיוע
והמשכה תחלה מלמעלה כי אלמלא עוזרו כו'... וסבירא ליה לרבי יוחנן
שדבר תורה הוא קנין גמור, שמשנמשך מ"ד זה הרי בודאי יהיה העלאת
מ"ן שהוא סוד הקנין והיציאה מרשות לרשות.

Rabbi Yochanan rules that Scripturally, money effects the sale. The Chasidic interpretation: At certain times, the purchaser will give the money prior to seizing the item. G-d works the same way; at times He will inspire us to reciprocate. To elicit an earthly awakening, man needs help from on High, for if G-d would not help him, he would not be able to arise... Rabbi Yochanan maintains that Scripturally [giving money alone] already completes the sale, namely, that when G-d sends His inspiration, it is certain that man will reciprocate and transfer ownership of this world to G-d.

6

SHAVUOT

The More the Merrier

Why Judaism Has 613 Commandments

Student Manual

PARSHA OVERVIEW
Shavuot

The Torah was given by G-d to the Jewish people on Mount Sinai more than 3300 years ago. Every year on the holiday of Shavuot we renew our acceptance of G-d's gift, and G-d "re-gives" the Torah.

The word Shavuot means "weeks." It marks the completion of the seven-week counting period between Passover and Shavuot.

The giving of the Torah was a far-reaching spiritual event—one that touched the essence of the Jewish soul for all times. Our sages have compared it to a wedding between G-d and the Jewish people. Shavuot also means "oaths," for on this day G-d swore eternal devotion to us, and we in turn pledged everlasting loyalty to Him.

In ancient times, two wheat loaves would be offered in Holy Temple. It was also at this time that people would begin to bring bikkurim, *their first and choicest fruits, to thank G-d for Israel's bounty.*

The holiday of Shavuot is a two-day holiday, beginning at sundown of the 5th of Sivan and lasting until nightfall of the 7th of Sivan. (In Israel it is a one-day holiday, ending at nightfall of the 6th of Sivan.)

- Women and girls light holiday candles to usher in the holiday, on both the first and second evenings of the holidays.

- It is customary to stay up all night learning Torah on the first night of Shavuot.

- All men, women and children should go to the synagogue on the first day of Shavuot to hear the reading of the Ten Commandments.

- As on other holidays, special meals are eaten, and no "work" may be performed.

- It is customary to eat dairy foods on Shavuot. Among other reasons, this commemorates the fact that upon receiving the Torah, including thekosher laws, the Jewish people could not cook meat in their pots, which had yet to be rendered kosher.

- On the second day of Shavuot, the Yizkor memorial service is recited.

- Some communities read the Book of Ruth publicly, as King David—whose passing occurred on this day—was a descendant of Ruth the Moabite.

1. The Development of 613

Primordial Mitzvot

TEXT 1A

Rabbi Moshe ben Maimon
(Maimonides, Rambam)
1135–1204

Halachist, philosopher, author, and physician. Maimonides was born in Cordoba, Spain. After the conquest of Cordoba by the Almohads, he fled Spain and eventually settled in Cairo, Egypt. There, he became the leader of the Jewish community and served as court physician to the vizier of Egypt. He is most noted for authoring the *Mishneh Torah*, an encyclopedic arrangement of Jewish law, and for his philosophical work, *Guide for the Perplexed*.

Maimonides, Mishneh Torah Laws of Kings 9:1-2

על ששה דברים נצטווה אדם הראשון: על עבודה זרה, ועל ברכת השם, ועל שפיכות דמים, ועל גילוי עריות, ועל הגזל, ועל הדינים. אף על פי שכולן הן קבלה בידינו ממשה רבינו והדעת נוטה להן, מכלל דברי תורה יראה שעל אלו נצטוה.

הוסיף לנח אבר מן החי ... נמצאו שבע מצות.

Six precepts were commanded to Adam:

The prohibitions against

1. Worshipping false gods

2. Blasphemy

3. Murder

4. Incest and adultery

5. Theft

6. The command to establish laws and courts of justice.

Even though we have received all of these commands from Moses and, [furthermore,] they are concepts which intellect itself tends to accept, it is evident from *the Torah's words that Adam was commanded concerning them.*

To Noach [G-d] added the prohibition against eating flesh from a living animal ... Thus there are seven mitzvot.

TEXT 1B

Ibid 9:3

וכן היה הדבר בכל העולם, עד אברהם. בא אברהם ונצטוה יתר על אלו במילה והוא התפלל שחרית. ויצחק הפריש מעשר והוסיף תפלה אחרת לפנות היום. ויעקב הוסיף גיד הנשה והתפלל ערבית. ובמצרים נצטוה עמרם במצות יתירות, עד שבא משה רבינו ונשלמה תורה על ידו.

The matter was such throughout the world until Abraham. When Abraham arose, in addition to these, he was commanded regarding circumcision. He also would pray the morning service.

Isaac separated tithes and added an additional prayer service before sunset. Jacob added the prohibition against eating the sciatic nerve and would pray the evening service. In Egypt, Amram was commanded regarding other mitzvot. *Ultimately, Moses came and the Torah was completed by him.*

Voluntary Fulfillment

TEXT 2A

Bereishit (Genesis) 26:5

עֵקֶב אֲשֶׁר שָׁמַע אַבְרָהָם בְּקֹלִי וַיִּשְׁמֹר מִשְׁמַרְתִּי מִצְוֹתַי חֻקּוֹתַי וְתוֹרֹתָי:

Because Abraham hearkened to My voice, and kept My charge, My commandments, My statutes, and My instructions.

TEXT 2B

Rabbi Shlomo Yitschaki
(Rashi)
1040–1105
Most noted biblical and Talmudic commentator. Born in Troyes, France, Rashi studied in the famed *yeshivot* of Mainz and Worms. His commentaries on the Pentateuch and the Talmud, which focus on the straightforward meaning of the text, have appeared in virtually every edition of the Talmud and Bible.

Rashi ad loc.

"וישמר משמרתי". גזרות להרחקה על אזהרות שבתורה, כגון שניות לעריות ושבות לשבת.

"מצותי". דברים שאילו לא נכתבו ראויין הם להצטוות כגון גזל ושפיכות דמים.

"חקותי". דברים שיצר הרע ואומות העולם משיבין עליהם כגון אכילת חזיר ולבישת שעטנז שאין טעם בדבר אלא גזירת המלך וחקותיו על עבדיו.

"ותורתי". להביא תורה שבעל פה, הלכה למשה מסיני.

And kept My charge." [Referring to Rabbinic] ordinances to distance [himself] from transgressing the warnings in the Torah, e.g. secondary prohibitions to prevent incest from occurring, and the enactments to safeguard the prohibitions of the Sabbath.

"My commandments." [Referring to] things, which, had they not been written, would have been fit to be commanded, e.g. [prohibitions against] robbery and bloodshed.

"My statutes." [Referring to] things that the evil inclination and the nations of the world argue against, e.g. [the prohibitions against] eating pork and wearing garments of wool and linen for which no reason [is given], but [which are] the decree of the King and His statutes over His subjects.

"And My instructions." To include the Oral Law, the laws given to Moses from Sinai.

Examples

TEXT 3

Midrash Hagadol, Bereishit ad loc.

אמר רב קיים אברהם אבינו כל התורה כולה שנאמר "וישמר משמרתי".
אמר ליה רב שימי בר חייא לרב ואימא שבע מצוות?
שבע מצוות ותו לא—והא הואי נמי מילה! אלא שבע מצוות ומילה.
אם כן "מצוותי ותורתי למה לי"?
אמר רב, ואי תימא רב אסי קיים אברהם אבינו אפלו עירובי תבשילין.
ויש אומרין אף עירובי בשר בחלב, ויביא ראיה מן "ויקח חמאה וחלב
ובן הבקר אשר עשה והוא עומד עליהם"—שמא יערבו בשר וחלב.

Rav said: Avraham fulfilled the entire Torah, as it is stated, "And he kept My charge."

Rabbi Simi bar Haia said to Rav, "We can say that this refers to the seven mitzvot?"

"No more than seven mitzvot?! There was also the mitzvah of brit milah!"

"Seven mitzvot and milah."

Rav said (others suggest it was Rabbi Assi): Avraham fulfilled all the mitzvot, including eiruv tavshilin. Others state that he kept the laws of not mixing meat and milk as well. There is evidence in the verse, "And he took cream and milk and the calf that he had prepared, and he placed [them] before them, and he was standing over them"—lest they mix meat and milk.

TEXT 4A

Bereishit (Genesis) 27:3

וְעַתָּה שָׂא נָא כֵלֶיךָ תֶּלְיְךָ וְקַשְׁתֶּךָ וְצֵא הַשָּׂדֶה וְצוּדָה לִּי צָיִד:

So, now, sharpen your implements, your sword [and take] your bow, and go forth to the field, and hunt game for me.

TEXT 4B

Rashi ad loc.

"שא נא"... חדד סכינך ושחוט יפה, שלא תאכילני נבלה.

"**S**harpen your knife and slaughter proper-ly."… Sharpen your knife and slaughter it well, lest you feed me an animal not properly slaughtered.

Tribes and Mitzvot

TEXT 5A

Bereishit (Genesis) 43:16

וַיַּרְא יוֹסֵף אִתָּם אֶת בִּנְיָמִין וַיֹּאמֶר לַאֲשֶׁר עַל בֵּיתוֹ הָבֵא אֶת הָאֲנָשִׁים הַבָּיְתָה וּטְבֹחַ טֶבַח וְהָכֵן כִּי אִתִּי יֹאכְלוּ הָאֲנָשִׁים בַּצָּהֳרָיִם:

When Joseph saw Benjamin with them, he said to the overseer of his house, "Bring the men into the house and [give orders] to slaughter an animal and to prepare, for the men will eat with me at lunch."

TEXT 6

Babylonian Talmud
A literary work of monumental proportions that draws upon the legal, spiritual, intellectual, ethical, and historical traditions of Judaism. The 37 tractates of the Babylonian Talmud contain the teachings of the Jewish sages from the period after the destruction of the 2nd Temple through the 5th century CE. It has served as the primary vehicle for the transmission of the Oral Law and the education of Jews over the centuries; it is the entry point for all subsequent legal, ethical, and theological Jewish scholarship.

Talmud Tractate Chulin 91a

מאי דכתיב "וטבוח טבח והכן"? פרע להם בית השחיטה.
רש"י: שלא יאמרו בשר הנחירה אני אוכל, לפי שבני יעקב שומרי מצוות
היו, דאף על פי שלא ניתנה תורה, מקובלים היו כן מאבותיהם.

What is the meaning of the verse, "And slaughter the animals and prepare the meat?" [It means] uncover for them the place of the slaughter.

Rashi: So that the brothers would not claim that the animals were improperly slaughtered. The sons of Jacob observed the mitzvot, for although the Torah had not yet been given, they possessed such a tradition from their fathers.

Subsequent Generations

TEXT 7A

Shemot (Exodus) 6:20

וַיִּקַּח עַמְרָם אֶת יוֹכֶבֶד דֹּדָתוֹ לוֹ לְאִשָּׁה וַתֵּלֶד לוֹ אֶת אַהֲרֹן וְאֶת מֹשֶׁה
וּשְׁנֵי חַיֵּי עַמְרָם שֶׁבַע וּשְׁלֹשִׁים וּמְאַת שָׁנָה:

Amram took Jochebed, his aunt, as his wife, and she bore him Aaron and Moses, and the years of Amram's life were one hundred thirty seven years.

TEXT 7B

Rashi ad loc.

"יוכבד דודתו". אחות אבוהי, בת לוי אחות קהת.

"Jochebed, his aunt." [Onkelos renders:] His father's sister, the daughter of Levi, the sister of Kehath.

The Arrival of 613

TEXT 8

Talmud Tractate Makot 23b-24a

דרש רבי שמלאי: שש מאות ושלש עשרה מצות נאמרו לו למשה שלש
מאות וששים וחמש לאוין ... ומאתים וארבעים ושמונה עשה ... אמר
רב המנונא: מאי קרא? "תורה צוה לנו משה מורשה"—תורה בגימטריא
שית מאה וחד סרי, הוי [ועוד] אנכי ולא יהיה לך מפי הגבורה שמענום.

Rabbi Simlai preached: Six hundred and thirteen precepts were communicated to Moses, three hundred and sixty-five negative precepts... and two hundred and forty-eight positive precepts...

Said Rabbi Hamnuna: What is the scriptural support for this? [It is the verse,] "Moses commanded us Torah, an inheritance [of the congregation of Jacob]." The word "Torah" equals six hundred and eleven in letter value. It follows that "Moses commanded us 611" and an additional two commandments] "I am [the Lord your G-d]" and "You shall have no [other gods]" we heard from the mouth of the Almighty Himself.

2. The Explanation of Rabbi Chanania ben Akashya

A Chance to do it Right

TEXT 9A

Talmud Tractate Makot ibid.

רבי חנניא בן עקשיא אומר: רצה הקדוש ברוך הוא לזכות את ישראל, לפיכך הרבה להם תורה ומצות. שנאמר "ה' חפץ למען צדקו יגדיל תורה ויאדיר".

Rabbi Chananiah ben Akashia says: The Holy One, blessed be He, wished to make Israel meritorious, therefore He gave them the law [to study] and commandments [to do] in abundant measure, as is stated, "G-d desired, for His righteousness sake, to make the law great and glorious."

TEXT 9B

Maimonides, Pirush Hamishnayot Makot 3:16

מעקרי האמונה בתורה כשיקיים אדם מצוה מתרי"ג מצות כראוי וכהוגן ולא ישתף עמה כוונה מכוונת העולם בשום פנים אלא שיעשה אותה לשמה מאהבה כמו שבארתי לך, הנה זכה בה לחיי העולם הבא. ועל זה

אמר רבי חנינא, כי המצות בהיותם הרבה אי אפשר שלא יעשה אדם בחייו אחת מהם על מתכונתה ושלמותה ובעשותו אותה המצוה תחיה נפשו באותו מעשה.

O ne of the fundamentals principles of our faith in the Torah is that when a person fulfills one of the 613 mitzvot as it should be, for absolutely no reason other than out of love for G-d, he merits the life of the World to Come. Regarding this Rabbi Chananiah says that because there are so many mitzvot, it is inevitable that a person will, at least once in his lifetime, fulfill one of them fully and properly. His soul will thus achieve life because of that mitzvah.

TEXT 10

Talmud Tractate Avodah Zara 18a:

תנו רבנן: כשחלה רבי יוסי בן קיסמא, הלך רבי חנינא בן תרדיון לבקרו... אמר לו: רבי, מה אני לחיי העולם הבא? אמר לו: כלום מעשה בא לידך? אמר לו: מעות של פורים נתחלפו לי במעות של צדקה וחלקתים לעניים, אמר לו: אם כן, מחלקך יהי חלקי ומגורלך יהי גורלי.

O ur Rabbis taught: When Rabbi Yosi ben Kisma was ill, Rabbi Chaninah ben Teradyon went to visit him... "Rabbi," said Rabbi Chaninah, "How do I stand with regard to the World to Come?"

"Is there any particular [special] act that you have done?" Rabbi Yosi inquired.

Rabbi Chaninah replied, "I once mistook [my] Purim funds for charity funds, and I distributed them to the poor [and when I discovered the error I did not reimburse myself]."

"In that case," said Rabbi Yosi, "I wish that your portion were my portion and your lot my lot."

TEXT 11

Maimonides, Ibid.

מה שיורה על העיקר הזה, מה ששאל ר' חנינא בן תרדיון "מה אני לחיי עולם הבא"? והשיבו המשיב "כלום בא מעשה לידך"? כלומר נזדמן לך לעשות מצוה כהוגן? השיבו כי נזדמנה לו מצות צדקה על דרך שלימות ככל מה שאפשר וזכה לחיי העולם הבא.

What demonstrates this principles is that which Rabbi Chaninah ben Tradyon asked, 'How do I stand with regard to the World to Come?' And he was answered, 'Is there any particular [special] act that you have done?!' Meaning, have you had the opportunity to do one mitzvah properly? He answered that he had fulfilled the mitzvah of charity to the utmost, and he merited the World to Come,

3. To Be Bound to Above

Binding Every Limb to G-d

TEXT 12A

Talmud, Tractate Makot, ibid.

דרש רבי שמלאי: שש מאות ושלש עשרה מצות נאמרו לו למשה...
ומאתים וארבעים ושמונה עשה כנגד איבריו של אדם.

Rabbi Simla'i said: 613 commandments were communicated to Moses... 248 positive commandments corresponding to the amount of limbs a person has.

TEXT 12B

Zohar vol. 1 p. 170b

Zohar
The seminal work of Kabbalah, Jewish mysticism. The Zohar is a mystical commentary on the Torah, written in Aramaic and Hebrew. According to Arizal, the Zohar contains the teachings of Rabbi Shimon bar Yocha'i who lived in the Land of Israel during the 2nd century. The Zohar has become one of the indispensable texts of traditional Judaism, alongside and nearly equal in stature to the Mishnah and Talmud.

דאית בבר נש רמ"ח שייפין לקבל רמ"ח פקודין דאורייתא... ואית בבר
נש שס"ה גידין ולקבלהון שס"ה פקודין דלאו אינון אתיהיבו למעבד...

A person has 248 limbs in order to receive the 248 positive commandments... and a person has 365 sinews corresponding to the 365 negative commandments.

TEXT 13

Rabbi Avraham Danziger, Kitzur Sefer Charedim:

מצות עשה מן התורה התלויות בעיניים: 1. להסתכל בציצית דכתיב
"וראיתם אותו וזכרתם" - ראייה מביאה לידי זכירה, וזכירה מביאה
לידי עשייה... 3. לבכות על אדם כשר שמת שנאמר: "ואחיכם כל בית
ישראל יבכו את השריפה", וזהו מכלל אהבת תלמיד חכם.

מצות לא תעשה מן התורה התלויות בעיניים: 1. אסור להסתכל בעריות
לשם זנות, שנאמר: "ולא תתורו וכו', אחרי עיניכם" כו'. 2. ואפילו שלא
לשם זנות, אלא שנהנה בראייתו, עובר בלאו שנאמר: "ונשמרת מכל
דבר רע". והשמר הוא לאו, דמכח זה יבא לידי תאווה וקרי. 3. שלא
להסתכל בעבודה זרה, והוא בכלל שנאמר: "אל תפנו אל האלילים" כו'.
4. הגאוה הוא תלוי בלב וגם בעינים, שנאמר: "גבה עינים" וכו', והוא
בכלל לאו ד"לא תתורו אחרי עיניכם".

מצות עשה מדברי סופרים התלויות בעיניים: 1. צריך שיסגור עיניו
בשעה שמתפלל מפחד השכינה העומדת לנגדו, או שיתפלל מתוך
הסידור. 2. בעת ענית קדושה ישא עיניו מעט למרום. 3. שיסתכל
לפעמים לשמים, כמה שכתוב "כי אראה שמים וכו', מה אנוש" כו',
וכן ישים מחשבה זו בלבו בעת הסתכלות. 4. מדרכי ענוה שיהיה שח
עיניים, שנאמר: "ושח עינים יושיע".

Positive Biblical commandments which involve the eyes:

*1. To look at the tzitzit, as it says, "And you will
see it and you will remember them." Seeing leads to
remembering, and remembering leads to action.*

*2. To not say by heart those things which are
in Scripture...*

3. *To cry over the death of a decent person, as it says, "And your brothers, the house of Israel, will cry over the tragedy." This is part of [the mitzvah] to love a Torah scholar.*

Negative Biblical commandments which involve the eyes:

1. It is forbidden to gaze at women lasciviously, as it says "And you will not stray after your eyes."...

3. To not look at idolatry, which is part of, "Do not turn to the gods."

4. Arrogance involves the heart as well as the eyes, as it says, "One whose eyes are raised up high." This is part of, "You shall not stray after your eyes."

Positive and negative Rabbninic injunctions that involve the eyes:

1. One should close their eyes during prayer, out of awe of the Divine Presence before them, or alternatively, pray from a siddur.

2. While responding during the kedushah recital, one should raise their eyes slightly to Heaven.

3. He should look to Heaven occasionally, as it says, "When I see your heavens... what is man..." He should have this thought in mind while he gazes upwards.

4. It is a mark of humility to have lowered eyes, as it says, "He will save a humble person."

Every Area of Life

TEXT 14

Midrash Tanchuma, Shelach §15

לא הניח דבר בעולם שלא נתן בו מצוה לישראל. יצא לחרוש – 'לא
תחרוש בשור וחמור'. לזרוע – 'לא תזרע כרמך כלאים'. לקצור – 'כי
תקצר קצירך בשדה'. בעיסה – 'ראשית עריסותיכם'. שחט – ונתן
לכהן זרוע לחיים וקיבה. שחט חיה ועוף – ושפך את דמו וכסהו
בעפר. קבר מת – 'לא תתגודדו'. מגלח שער ראש – 'לא תקיפו פאת
ראשכם'. בנה בית – 'ועשית מעקה' ומזוזה. נתכסה בטלית – 'ועשו
להם ציצית'.

Tanchuma
A Midrashic work bearing
the name of Rabbi Tanchuma,
a 4th-century Talmudic
sage quoted often in
this work. This Midrash
provides textual exegeses
and stories, expounds upon
the biblical narrative, and
develops and illustrates
moral principles. *Tanchuma*
is unique in that many of its
sections commence with a
halachic discussion, which
subsequently leads into
non-halachic teachings.

There is nothing in this world in which G-d did not give the Jewish people a mitzvah. When one goes out to plough, "Do not plough an ox together with a donkey." To sow, "Do not sow kila'im [mixed seeds] in your vineyard." To harvest, "When you shall reap your harvest in the field." For dough, "The first of your dough." To slaughter, "He shall give the kohen the foreleg, the jaws, and the maw." When slaughtering animals and birds, "And when he sheds its blood, he shall cover the blood with dust." When burying the dead, "You shall not cut yourselves." When getting a haircut, "You shall not round off the corner of your head." When he builds a house, "You shall make a fence," and [the mitzvah of] mezuzah. When donning a garment, "And you shall make tzitzit for them."

TEXT 15

Rabbi Menachem Mendel Schneerson
1902–1994

The towering Jewish leader of the 20th century, known as "the Lubavitcher Rebbe," or simply as "the Rebbe." Born in southern Ukraine, the Rebbe escaped Nazi occupied Europe, arriving in the U.S. in June 1941. The Rebbe inspired and guided the revival of traditional Judaism after the European devastation, impacting virtually every Jewish community the world over. The Rebbe often emphasized that the performance of just one additional good deed could usher in the era of Mashiach. The Rebbe's scholarly talks and writings have been printed in more than 200 volumes.

The Lubavitcher Rebbe, Likutei Sichot vol. 17 p. 412

המשנה מסבירה "רצה הקדוש ברוך הוא לזכות את ישראל", "לזכות" הוא מלשון "זיכוך". הרצון של הקדוש ברוך הוא הוא לא (רק) שהיהודים יגיעו לידי ביטול לאלוקות, אלא שיפעל בהם (גם) הענין של זיכוך. תוכן הביטול הוא שנאבדת המציאות של האדם ועל ידי זה הוא נעשה דבוק לאלוקות ... [אולם] הענין של זיכוך הוא, שהאדם עצמו – איבריו וגידיו – מזדככים ונעשים דבר אחד עם אלוקות ... והיות שהקדוש ברוך הוא רוצה שהיהודי יפעל בעצמו את ענין הזיכוך, לפיכך "הרבה" להם תורה ומצוות – ויש כזה ריבוי והתחלקות בתורה ומצוות, משום שלכל מצוה יש ענין מיוחד שפועלת זיכוך בכח ואבר וגיד מסויים.

The Mishnah explains that "G-d wanted to give merit to Israel." The word "merit" (לזכות) is related to the word for "refinement" (זיכוך). G-d wanted not only that Jews would achieve *bittul [a sense of nullification]* to G-dliness, but that this would also effect in them refinement.

The idea of bittul *is that the person loses his sense of autonomy and, in this manner he becomes attached to G-d... The idea of refinement is that the very person— his limbs and his sinews—become one with G-dliness... Now, because G-d wanted that the Jew should effect within himself this refinement, He "multiplied" the Torah and* mitzvot. *There are many and varied* mitzvot, *because each mitzvah has a unique aspect that effects the refinement of a particular limb.*

Conclusion—A Healthy Soul in a Healthy Body

TEXT 16A

The Lubavitcher Rebbe, Igrot Kodesh vol. 12 p. 226

בעת רצון אזכיר אותה על הציון הקדוש של כ"ק אדמו"ר לברכה לבריאות טובה, ומן הסתם שומעת היא קידוש והבדלה, וגם טועמת מיין הקידוש, ולפי מנהג ישראל, טובלת את האצבעות בנשאר מיין ההבדלה ומעבירה אותן על העינים - אשר לפי המובא בספרים, זו סגולה למאור העיניים של האדם.

In response to someone who had asked for a blessing for better vision: I will mention you for blessing for good health at an auspicious time at the resting place of the [Previous] Rebbe. I assume that you hear kiddush *and* havdalah, *taste the wine of* kiddush, *and (as per Jewish custom) dip your fingers in the wine leftover from* havdalah *and then pass the fingers over the eyes. According to the Holy Books, this is a* segulah *for one's vision.*

TEXT 16B

Igrot Kodesh vol. 19 p. 102

כיון שבאיש הישראלי, הגשמיות והרוחניות יחד יהלכו, ואמרו חכמינו
זכרונם לברכה: 'היקום אשר ברגליהם זה ממונו של אדם שמעמידו על
רגליו', מהנכון שירבה בצדקה כפשוטה, ובייחוד למוסדות שמתעסקים
בחינוך בני ישראל על טהרת הקודש, שגם הם בבחינת רגל דקומה
הכללית של בני ישראל.

In response to someone who had asked for a blessing for healthy legs: For a Jew, the spiritual goes hand in hand with the physical. The Sages said [that the verse which states] "And all the possessions at their feet"—refers to one's money, which puts him on his feet. Accordingly, it is fitting for him to increase in charity in its literal sense, and specifically, charity to organizations that are involved with pure Jewish education, for they too are the legs on which the entire Jewish people stands.

TEXT 16C

Igrot Kodesh vol. 7 p. 19

כידוע מאמר רבותינו זכרונם לברכה אשר רמ"ח מצוות עשה הם כנגד
רמ"ח אברים של האדם ושס"ה מצוות לא תעשה כנגד שס"ה גידי
האדם. פשוט הדבר שאין זה רק דמיון במספר, אלא שאברי האדם
מקבלים חיות על ידי עשיית מצוות עשה וגידי האדם [פועלים
פעולתם התקינה בתור] צנורות טהורים ובלתי מקולקלים חס ושלום
בהליכת הדם, על ידי שמירת שס"ה לא תעשה. וכמובן אשר הרוחניות
והגשמיות של איש הישראלי הם אינם שני דברים נפרדים, אלא דבר
אחד ממש והא בהא תליא.

It is well known the statement of our Sages that the 248 positive commandments correspond to the 248 limbs of the human being, and the 365 negative commandments correspond to the 365 veins of the human being. This relationship is obviously not just a similarity in number, rather [the following:] One's limbs receive their life-force through the observance of the positive mitzvot and the veins operate as flawless conduits for the blood through the observance of the 365 negative commandments. A Jew's spiritual and physical lives are one and the same, and depend on each other.

TEXT 17

Midrash Yalkut Shimoni, Mishlei §935

אמר הקדוש ברוך הוא לישראל: שמרו רמ"ח מצוות עשה שמסרתי
לכם, ואני אשמור רמ"ח אברים שבכל אחד ואחד מכם. הדא הוא
דכתיב "שמור מצותי וחיה."

G-d said to the Jewish people: Guard the 248
positive commandments that I am giving over
to you, and I will guard the 248 limbs within
each one of you. This is what is meant by the verse,
"Guard My commandments and live."

Yalkut Shimoni

A Midrash that covers the
entire Biblical text. Its
material is collected from
all over rabbinic literature,
including the Babylonian
and Jerusalem Talmuds and
various ancient Midrashic
texts. It contains several
passages from Midrashim
that have been lost, as well
as different versions of
existing Midrashim. It is
unclear when and by whom
this Midrash was redacted.

My Mitzvah

TEXT 18

Rabbi Yosef Yitzchak Schneersohn of Lubavitch,
Sefer Hamaamarim 5708 p. 240 fn 6

מה שמצינו כמה מאמרי חכמינו זכרונם לברכה שהיו זהירים במצוה
פרטית ביחוד הוא ... על פי מה שכתוב בעץ חיים שער ק"נ ... והמצוה
היתה לפי מקום תליית נשמתו בנשמת אדם הראשון.

As for why so many Sages were focused on
one particular mitzvah... this is because that
mitzvah corresponds to the part of Adam's
soul from which this sage's soul stems.

**Rabbi Yosef Yitschak
Schneersohn**
(Rayats, Frierdiker Rebbe,
Previous Rebbe)
1880–1950

Chasidic rebbe, prolific writer,
and Jewish activist. Rabbi
Yosef Yitschak, the 6th leader
of the Chabad movement,
actively promoted Jewish
religious practice in Soviet
Russia and was arrested for
these activities. After his
release from prison and exile,
he settled in Warsaw, Poland,
from where he fled Nazi
occupation, and arrived in
New York in 1940. Settling in
Brooklyn, Rabbi Schneersohn
worked to revitalize American
Jewish life. His son-in law,
Rabbi Menachem Mendel
Schneerson, succeeded
him as the leader of the
Chabad movement.

7

NASSO

In Search of the Eighth Note

A Discussion on Music

Student Manual

PARSHA OVERVIEW
Nasso

Completing the headcount of the Children ofIsrael taken in the Sinai Desert, a total of 8,580 Levite men between the ages of 30and 50 are counted in a tally of those who will be doing the actual work of transporting the Tabernacle.

G-d communicates to Moses the law of the sotah, the wayward wife suspected of unfaithfulness to her husband. Also given is the law of the nazir, who forswears wine, lets his or her hair grow long, and is forbidden to become contaminated through contact with a dead body. Aaron and his descendants, the kohanim, are instructed on how to bless the people of Israel.

The leaders of the twelve tribes of Israel each bring their offerings for theinauguration of the altar. Although their gifts are identical, each is brought on a different day and is individually described by the Torah.

1. The Levite Job

Desert Schleppers

TEXT 1A

Bamidbar 4:15

וְכִלָּה אַהֲרֹן וּבָנָיו לְכַסֹּת אֶת הַקֹּדֶשׁ וְאֶת כָּל כְּלֵי הַקֹּדֶשׁ בִּנְסֹעַ הַמַּחֲנֶה וְאַחֲרֵי כֵן יָבֹאוּ בְנֵי קְהָת לָשֵׂאת וְלֹא יִגְּעוּ אֶל הַקֹּדֶשׁ וָמֵתוּ אֵלֶּה מַשָּׂא בְנֵי קְהָת בְּאֹהֶל מוֹעֵד:

Aaron and his sons shall finish covering the Holy and all the vessels of the Holy when the camp is set to travel, and following that, the sons of Kehot shall come to carry [them], but they shall not touch the sacred objects for [then] they will die. These are the burden of the sons of Kehot for the Tent of Meeting.

TEXT 1B

Ibid. 4:24-26

זֹאת עֲבֹדַת מִשְׁפְּחֹת הַגֵּרְשֻׁנִּי לַעֲבֹד וּלְמַשָּׂא:
וְנָשְׂאוּ אֶת יְרִיעֹת הַמִּשְׁכָּן וְאֶת אֹהֶל מוֹעֵד מִכְסֵהוּ וּמִכְסֵה הַתַּחַשׁ אֲשֶׁר עָלָיו מִלְמָעְלָה וְאֶת מָסַךְ פֶּתַח אֹהֶל מוֹעֵד:
וְאֵת קַלְעֵי הֶחָצֵר וְאֶת מָסַךְ פֶּתַח שַׁעַר הֶחָצֵר אֲשֶׁר עַל הַמִּשְׁכָּן וְעַל הַמִּזְבֵּחַ סָבִיב וְאֵת מֵיתְרֵיהֶם וְאֶת כָּל כְּלֵי עֲבֹדָתָם וְאֵת כָּל אֲשֶׁר יֵעָשֶׂה לָהֶם וְעָבָדוּ:

This is the service of the Gershonite families to serve and to carry.

They shall carry the curtains of the Mishkan and the Tent of Meeting, its covering and the tachash skin covering overlaid upon it, and the screen for the entrance to the Tent of Meeting.

The hangings of the courtyard, the screen at the entrance of the gate of the courtyard which is around the Mishkan and the altar, their ropes, all the work involved, and everything that is made for them, and thus shall they serve.

TEXT 1C

Ibid. 4:31-33

וְזֹאת מִשְׁמֶרֶת מַשָּׂאָם לְכָל עֲבֹדָתָם בְּאֹהֶל מוֹעֵד קַרְשֵׁי הַמִּשְׁכָּן וּבְרִיחָיו וְעַמּוּדָיו וַאֲדָנָיו:

וְעַמּוּדֵי הֶחָצֵר סָבִיב וְאַדְנֵיהֶם וִיתֵדֹתָם וּמֵיתְרֵיהֶם לְכָל כְּלֵיהֶם וּלְכֹל עֲבֹדָתָם וּבְשֵׁמֹת תִּפְקְדוּ אֶת כְּלֵי מִשְׁמֶרֶת מַשָּׂאָם:

זֹאת עֲבֹדַת מִשְׁפְּחֹת בְּנֵי מְרָרִי לְכָל עֲבֹדָתָם בְּאֹהֶל מוֹעֵד בְּיַד אִיתָמָר בֶּן אַהֲרֹן הַכֹּהֵן:

This is the charge of their burden for all their service in the Tent of Meeting: the planks of the Mishkan, its bars, its pillars, and its sockets.

The pillars of the surrounding courtyard, their sockets, their pegs, and their ropes, all their implements for all the work involved. You shall designate by name the implements charged to them for their burden.

This is the service of the families of the sons of Merari for all their service in the Tent of Meeting, which was under the supervision of Itamar, the son of Aaron the kohen.

TEXT 2A

Ibid 4:47

מִבֶּן שְׁלֹשִׁים שָׁנָה וָמַעְלָה וְעַד בֶּן חֲמִשִּׁים שָׁנָה כָּל הַבָּא לַעֲבֹד עֲבֹדַת עֲבֹדָה וַעֲבֹדַת מַשָּׂא בְּאֹהֶל מוֹעֵד:

From the age of thirty years and upward, until the age of fifty years, who are fit to perform the service for the service and the work of carrying, in the Tent of Meeting.

QUESTION FOR DISCUSSION

What do you think "service for the service" means?

TEXT 2B

Rashi ad loc.

"עבדת עבדה". הוא השיר במצלתים וכנורות, שהיא עבודה
לעבודה אחרת.

"To perform the service for the service."
This refers to the music with cymbals
and harps, which is a service for another service.

Rabbi Shlomo Yitschaki
(Rashi)
1040–1105

Most noted biblical and
Talmudic commentator.
Born in Troyes, France,
Rashi studied in the famed
yeshivot of Mainz and
Worms. His commentaries
on the Pentateuch and the
Talmud, which focus on the
straightforward meaning
of the text, have appeared
in virtually every edition
of the Talmud and Bible.

Musical Instruments

TEXT 3

Divrei Hayamim I (I Chronicles) 15:16

וַיֹּאמֶר דָּוִיד לְשָׂרֵי הַלְוִיִּם לְהַעֲמִיד אֶת אֲחֵיהֶם הַמְשֹׁרְרִים בִּכְלֵי שִׁיר
נְבָלִים וְכִנֹּרוֹת וּמְצִלְתָּיִם מַשְׁמִיעִים לְהָרִים בְּקוֹל לְשִׂמְחָה:

And David said to the leaders of the Levites to
station their brethren, the singers, with musical instruments, psalteries, and harps and
cymbals, resounding to raise a voice in joy.

TEXT 4

Mishnah Tractate Arachin 2:3, 6

Mishnah

The first authoritative work of Jewish law that was codified in writing. The Mishnah contains the oral traditions that were passed down from teacher to student; it supplements, clarifies, and systematizes the commandments of the Torah. Due to the continual persecution of the Jewish people, it became increasingly difficult to guarantee that these traditions would not be forgotten. Rabbi Yehudah Hanasi therefore redacted the Mishnah at the end of the 2nd century. It serves as the foundation for the Talmud.

אין פוחתין משני נבלין ולא מוסיפין על ששה אין פוחתין משני חלילין
ולא מוסיפין על שנים עשר...
אין פוחתין משנים עשר לוים עומדים על הדוכן ומוסיפין עד לעולם אין
קטן נכנס לעזרה לעבודה אלא בשעה שהלוים עומדים בשיר ולא היו
אומרים בנבל וכנור אלא בפה כדי ליתן תבל בנעימה.

The Levite orchestra was not to have less than two harps, or more than six, nor less than two flutes, or more than twelve…

There was never to be less than twelve Levites standing on the platform, and their number could be increased into infinity. No minor could enter the court of the Sanctuary to take part in the service except when the Levites stood up to sing. Nor did they join in the singing with harp and lyre, but with the mouth alone, to add flavor to the music.

Secret Sauce

TEXT 5

Talmud Tractate Yoma 38a-b

ואלו לגנאי... הוגרס בן לוי היה יודע פרק בשיר ולא רצה ללמד...
תניא: כשהוא נותן קולו בנעימה מכניס גודלו לתוך פיו, ומניח אצבעו בין
הנימין, עד שהיו אחיו הכהנים נזקרים בבת ראש לאחוריהם. (נרתעין
מהכרעת הקול. –רש"י)

Babylonian Talmud
A literary work of monumental proportions that draws upon the legal, spiritual, intellectual, ethical, and historical traditions of Judaism. The 37 tractates of the Babylonian Talmud contain the teachings of the Jewish sages from the period after the destruction of the 2nd Temple through the 5th century CE. It has served as the primary vehicle for the transmission of the Oral Law and the education of Jews over the centuries; it is the entry point for all subsequent legal, ethical, and theological Jewish scholarship.

And these were mentioned to their shame... Hygros, son [of the tribe] of Levi, knew a cadence in song but would not teach it...

It was taught: When he tuned his voice to a trill, he would put his thumb into his mouth and place his finger [on the division line] between the two parts of the moustache, so that his brethren, the priests, staggered backward with a sudden movement. (From the force of the sound. –Rashi)

Rare Instruments

TEXT 6

Talmud Tractate Arachin 10b-11a

מגריפה היתה במקדש, עשרה נקבים היו בה, כל אחד ואחד מוציא
עשרה מיני זמר, נמצאת כולה מוציאה מאה מיני זמר. במתניתא תנא:
היא אמה וגבוה אמה, וקתא יוצא הימנה ועשרה נקבים היו בה, כל אחד
מוציא מאה מיני זמר, נמצאת כולה מוציאה אלף מיני זמר.

There was a magrefah (a certain musical instrument) in the Sanctuary; it had ten holes,
each of which produced ten different kinds of
sounds. It follows that the entire instrument produced
one hundred kinds of sounds.

A Tanna *taught: It was one cubit long, one cubit high;
from it projected a handle which had ten holes. Each
of them produced one hundred kinds of sounds; it follows that the entire instrument produced one thousand
kinds of sounds.*

TEXT 7

Rabbi Yehudah Halevi, Kuzari 2:64

אבל חכמת המוסיקא, חשוב באומה שהיא מכבדת הנגונים ומעמדת
אותם על הגדולים שבעם, והם בני לוי, מתעסקים בנגונים בבית הנכבד
בעתים הנכבדים, ולא הוצרכו להתעסק בצרכי הפרנסה במה שהיו
לוקחים מהמעשרות ולא היה להם עסק זולתי המוסיקא. והמלאכה
נכבדת אצל בני אדם, כאשר היא בעצמה אינה גרועה ולא פחותה,
והעם מחשיבות השרש וזכות הטבע כאשר הם.

Rabbi Yehudah Halevi
ca. 1075–1141

Born in Tudela, Spain;
rabbi, physician, and poet.
Rabbi Yehudah Halevi is
best known as the author of
the *Kuzari*, a philosophical
work, written in the form
of a discussion between
a Jew, a Christian, and a
Muslim before the King of the
Khazars. In addition to the
Kuzari, he wrote thousands
of poems, of which only a
few hundred survive today.

The art of music is prominent in a nation which respects songs and allocates them to the aristocracy of the people, namely the Levites, who engaged in song in the honored house at honored times. They did not need to engage in livelihood for they would receive the tithes, and they had no occupation but music. This craft is highly esteemed among mankind, as long as it is not abused and degraded, and the people preserve its original nobleness and purity.

2. Music throughout the Ages

In the Torah

TEXT 8A

Bereishit (Genesis) 4:21

וְשֵׁם אָחִיו יוּבָל הוּא הָיָה אֲבִי כָּל תֹּפֵשׂ כִּנּוֹר וְעוּגָב:

And his brother's name was Jubal; he was the father of all who grasp a lyre and a flute.

TEXT 8B

Shemot (Exodus) 15:20

וַתִּקַּח מִרְיָם הַנְּבִיאָה אֲחוֹת אַהֲרֹן אֶת הַתֹּף בְּיָדָהּ וַתֵּצֶאןָ כָל הַנָּשִׁים אַחֲרֶיהָ בְּתֻפִּים וּבִמְחֹלֹת:

Miriam, the prophetess, Aaron's sister, took a timbrel in her hand, and all the women came out after her with timbrels and with dances.

Prophets

TEXT 9A

Shmuel II 6:5

וְדָוִד וְכָל בֵּית יִשְׂרָאֵל מְשַׂחֲקִים לִפְנֵי ה' בְּכֹל עֲצֵי בְרוֹשִׁים וּבְכִנֹּרוֹת
וּבִנְבָלִים וּבְתֻפִּים וּבִמְנַעַנְעִים וּבְצֶלְצֶלִים:

And David and all the house of Israel made merry with all [manner of instruments of] cypress wood, and with harps, and with psalteries, and with timbrels, and with sistra, and with cymbals.

TEXT 9B

Shmuel I 16:23

וְהָיָה בִּהְיוֹת רוּחַ אֱלֹקִים אֶל שָׁאוּל וְלָקַח דָּוִד אֶת הַכִּנּוֹר וְנִגֵּן בְּיָדוֹ וְרָוַח
לְשָׁאוּל וְטוֹב לוֹ וְסָרָה מֵעָלָיו רוּחַ הָרָעָה:

And it would be, that when the spirit of G-d was upon Saul, that David would take the harp, and would play with his hand, and Saul would be relieved, and it would be good for him, and the spirit of evil would depart from him.

TEXT 9C

Talmud Tractate Berachot 3b

כנור היה תלוי למעלה ממטתו של דוד, וכיון שהגיע חצות לילה בא רוח
צפונית ונושבת בו ומנגן מאליו, מיד היה עומד ועוסק בתורה עד שעלה
עמוד השחר.

A harp was hanging above David's bed. As soon as midnight arrived, a north wind came and blew upon it and it played of itself. He arose immediately and studied the Torah until the break of dawn.

Talmud

TEXT 10A

Talmud Tractate Megillah 32a

אמר רבי שפטיה אמר רבי יוחנן: כל הקורא בלא נעימה ושונה בלא
זמרה, עליו הכתוב אומר "וגם אני נתתי להם חקים לא טובים וגו'".

R abbi Shefatiah said in the name of Rabbi Yochanan: If one reads the Scripture without a melody or repeats the Mishnah without a tune, of him the Scripture says, "Wherefore I gave them also statutes that were not good, etc."

TEXT 10B

Tosafot ad loc.

"והשונה בלא זמרה". שהיו רגילין לשנות המשניות בזמרה לפי שהיו
שונין אותן על פה ועל ידי כך היו נזכרים יותר.

"Or repeats the Mishnah without a tune."
It was their practice to study Mishnah
with a tune for they would study them
orally [by heart], and the tunes would aide in memorizing the studies.

Tosafot
A collection of French and German Talmudic commentaries written during the 12th and 13th centuries. Among the most famous authors of *Tosafot* are Rabbi Ya'akov Tam, Rabbi Shimshon ben Avraham of Sens, and Rabbi Yitschak ("the Ri"). Printed in almost all editions of the Talmud, these commentaries are fundamental to basic Talmudic study.

3. The Philosophy of Jewish Music

TEXT 11

Rabbi Moshe ben Nachman
(Nachmanides, Ramban)
1194–1270

Scholar, philosopher, author and physician. Nachmanides was born in Spain and served as leader of Iberian Jewry. In 1263, he was summoned by King James of Aragon to a public disputation with Pablo Cristiani, a Jewish apostate. Though Nachmanides was the clear victor of the debate, he had to flee Spain because of the resulting persecution. He moved to Israel and helped reestablish communal life in Jerusalem. He authored a classic commentary on the Pentateuch and a commentary on the Talmud.

Nachmanides, Torat Ha'adam, Sha'ar Hagemul

אין בגשמיות דק כמוסיקא.

There is nothing more abstract in the material world than music.

Aids Concentration

TEXT 12

Rabbi Aharon Halevi of Barcelona, Sefer Hachinuch, §384

משרשי המצוה, לפי שבשעת הקרבן היו צריכין לכוון דעתם יפה בענינו כמו שידוע שהוא נפסל במחשבות ידועות, וגם כן צריך הקרבן כוונה שלמה לפני אדון הכל שציונו עליו, וגם כן בעת הצרה צריך האדם כיוון גדול בהתחננו לפי בוראו שירחם עליו ויצילהו מצרתו, ולכן נצטוו בתקיעת החצוצרות בעתים אלה. לפי שהאדם מהיותו בעל חומר צריך התעוררות גדול אל הדברים. כי הטבע מבלי מעיר יעמוד כישן, ואין דבר יעוררהו כמו קולות הנגון, ידוע הדבר, וכל שכן קול החצוצרות שהוא הקול הגדול שבכל כלי ניגון.

The reason for the mitzvah [of blowing trumpets in the Temple]: When a sacrifice is offered, the people involved were required to rid their minds of all thoughts, and focus upon it attentively, pointing their minds with intense concentration to G-d Who commanded the mitzvah. Similarly, during a time of trouble [when trumpets are blown], a person must be fully focused when pleading with G-d to have mercy and save him from all troubles. For this reason we are commanded to blow trumpets at these times. Since, naturally, a person is coarse, he needs to be driven; without motivation, a person would naturally lie idle. It is well known that there is nothing quite rousing like the strains of music, certainly so with the blasts of a trumpet which is the most powerful of musical instruments.

Sefer Hachinuch
A work on the biblical commandments. Four aspects of every mitzvah are discussed in this work: the definition of the mitzvah; ethical lessons that can be deduced from the mitzvah; basic laws pertaining to the observance of the mitzvah; and who is obligated to perform the mitzvah and when. The work was composed in the 13th century by an anonymous author who refers to himself as "the Levite of Barcelona." It has been widely thought that this referred to Rabbi Aharon Halevi of Barcelona (Re'ah); however, this view has been contested.

Lifts Depression

TEXT 13

Maimonides, Eight Chapters, chapter 5

צריך האדם שישתמש בכוחות נפשו כולם לפי הדעה שהצענו בפרק שלפני זה. וישים לנגד עיניו תכלית אחת והיא: השגת השם יתברך, כפי יכולת האדם לדעתו. ויהיו מעשיו כולם, תנועותיו ומנוחותיו וכל אמרי פיו מביאים אל התכלית הזאת, עד שלא יהיה במעשיו שום מעשה לבטלה, רצוני לומר: מעשה שלא יביא אל התכלית הזאת.

כגון זה, שיהא מכוון באכילתו ובשתייתו, ושנתו ויקיצתו, ותנועתו ומנוחתו, לבריאות גופו לבד. והחפץ בבריאות גופו, שתמצא הנפש כליה בריאים, שלמים. והתמסרה לחכמות, וקנות המעלות המידותיות והדבריות, עד שיגיע לאותה התכלית.

ועל פי היקש זה, אין כוונתו אותה שעה ההנאה בלבד, עד שיבחר במזון ובמשתה את הערב ביותר, וכן בשאר ההנהגה. אבל יכוון אל המועיל ביותר, בין שהוא ערב ובין שאינו ערב; או יכוון אל הערב ביותר מבחינת מדע הרפואה.

כמי שפסקה תאוותו למזון, ומעוררה במאכלי-תאווה ערבים, מתובלים. והוא הדין מי שהתתרגשה עליו מרה שחורה, ועמד והסירה בשמיעת הניגונים ובמיני הזמר, ובטיול בגינות ובבניינים נאים, ובישיבה עם צורות נאות וכיוצא בדברים שמרחיבים הנפש ומסירים הרהוריו הקודרים ממנה.

והמכוון בכל זה, שיבריא גופו, ותכלית בריאות גופו: לקנות חכמה. והוא הדין מי שטרח והתעסק בקנות הממון, תהיה תכליתו בקיבוצו שיוציאו למעלות, ושימצאהו לקיום גופו והמשך מציאותו, עד שיציג וידע את השם יתברך, מה שאפשר לדעתו.

It is the duty of man to subordinate all the faculties of his soul to his reason. He must keep his mind's eye fixed constantly upon one goal, namely, the attainment of the knowledge of G-d, as far as it is possible for mortal man to know Him. Consequently, one must so adjust all his actions, his whole conduct, and even his very words that they lead to this goal, in order that none of his deeds be aimless, and thus prevent the attainment of that end.

So, his only design in eating and drinking, sleeping and waking, moving about and resting, should be the preservation of bodily health, while, in turn, the reason for the latter is that the soul and its agencies may be in sound and perfect condition, so that he may readily acquire wisdom, and gain moral and intellectual virtues, all to the end that man may reach the highest goal of his endeavors. Accordingly, man will not direct his attention merely to obtain bodily enjoyment, choosing of food and drink and in all other matters only the most pleasurable, but he will seek out the most useful, being indifferent whether it be pleasurable or not.

There are, indeed, times when the pleasurable may be used from a curative point of view, as, for instance, when one suffers from loss of appetite, it may be stirred up by highly seasoned delicacies and pleasurable foods.

Similarly, one who suffers from melancholia may rid himself of it by listening to singing and all kinds

Rabbi Moshe ben Maimon
(Maimonides, Rambam)
1135–1204

Halachist, philosopher, author, and physician. Maimonides was born in Cordoba, Spain. After the conquest of Cordoba by the Almohads, he fled Spain and eventually settled in Cairo, Egypt. There, he became the leader of the Jewish community and served as court physician to the vizier of Egypt. He is most noted for authoring the *Mishneh Torah*, an encyclopedic arrangement of Jewish law, and for his philosophical work, *Guide for the Perplexed*.

of instrumental music, by strolling among beautiful gardens and edifices, by gazing upon beautiful pictures, and other things that enliven the mind and dissipate gloomy moods. The purpose of all this is to restore the healthful condition of the body, but the real object in maintaining the body in good health is to acquire wisdom.

Likewise, in the pursuit of wealth, the main design in its acquisition should be to expend it for noble purposes, and to employ it for the maintenance of the body and the preservation of life, so that its owner may obtain a knowledge of G-d, insofar as that is vouchsafed unto man.

A Lofty Wisdom

TEXT 14

Rabbi Yonatan Eybeschutz, Ya'arot Devash vol. 2 p 133b

מחכמת המוזיקא אין לדבר כי הוא חכמת השיר ובזה נבין כל ענייני הטעמים ונקוד השיר, השירים בתורה ונועם מליצת לוים וכדומה בכל פרטי דברים והם נגונים ישרים לשמח לבבות להסיר מרה שחורה ולקנות הנפש שמחה שיחול בה רוח אלוקה כמעשה הנביאים. ומה רב כחו של חכמה זו אשר כל מלאכי מעלה וגלגלי שמים כלם ינגנו וישירו בשיר ונגון נועם כפי סדר טוב הקולות וחצי קולות וכולם יש להם שרש בחכמת אמת וכל תנועה יש לה שרשים .

egarding the art of music, we need not even mention! The art of music opens a window to the cantillation marks and the songs in the Torah, as well as the music of the Levites. They are songs designed to gladden the heart and remove depression, instilling a sense of joy in the soul to facilitate a G-dly spirit, as was the habit of the prophets.

How great is the power of this art! All of the angels and celestial hosts raise their voices in song, in a harmonious pattern of full voices paired with shorter ones. All of these songs are rooted in the Wisdom of Truth, and each rhythm has a supernal root.

Rabbi Yonatan Eybeschutz
1690–1764
Talmudist, authority on Jewish law, and kabbalist. Recognized during his youth as a prodigy in Talmud, Rabbi Eybeshutz was appointed rabbinical magistrate of Prague, and later rabbi of Metz. In 1750, he was elected rabbi of Altona, Hamburg, and Wandsbek. He was surrounded by controversy after Rabbi Ya'akov Emden accused him of Sabbatean sympathies. 30 of his works were published, including *Urim Vetumim*, *Kereti Upeleti*, *Sar Ha'alef* on the *Code of Jewish Law*, and *Ye'arot Devash*, a collection of his sermons.

Pruning Obstacles

TEXT 15

Rabbi Yitzchak Abohav, Menorat Hama'or
Ner 3, Kelal 3, Chelek 1, Perek 3

Rabbi Yitschak Abohav
14th
century Preacher and author. Born in Spain, Rabbi Abohav, a businessman, was distressed over the lack of Jewish scholarship in his time. Toward the end of his life, therefore, he dedicated much time to preaching and writing. Abohav wrote *Menorat Hama'or*, a work on ethics based on the aggadic sections of the Talmud. The work became a popular household book in medieval Jewish homes.

מצאתי כתוב כי לכן נקראו הזמירות והשירים מזמורים מלשון לא
תזמור ולפי זה זמירות רוצה לומר זמורות שכשם שהמזמר בגפנים
יקוץ כל הזמורות ויניח מה שראוי לרטב כך הזמירות שאנו אומרים
קודם התפלה יסירו ויקוצו כל המכשולות והעוונות שיש לנו לפני השם
יתברך וכשתבא תפילתנו שתיהיה נשמעת ורצויה לפני השם.

have found it written that, for this reason, the songs and chants in prayer are called "zemirot": This word is connected with the Hebrew word *"pruning." Just as one prunes away the undesirables in his orchard and leaves the quality branches to grow, in this understanding, the song and praise we utter before prayers "prune" away the obstructions and sins that stand between us and G-d so that when our prayers ascend to G-d, they are acceptable and favorable before Him.*

·

Seven and Eight

TEXT 16A

Rabbi Yisroel Taub
1849–1920

Chasidic Rebbe, founder of the Modzitz Chasidic dynasty. Rabbi Taub succeeded his father as the leader of the Zvoliner Chasidim, moving to the town of Modrzyc, thus establishing a dynasty that carries that name. Rabbi Taub was a gifted musician and composed many melodies that are sung by his Chasidim and others until today. His teachings are collected in a work entitled *Divrei Yisroel*.

Rabbi Yisroel Taub, LaChasidim Mizmor p. 79

ידוע לחכמי הנגינה... היות וחכמת הנגינה והמוסיקה חצובה עמודיה שבעה, היינו שהיא בנויה על שבע מדריגות הקול מנמוך לגבוה ומגבוה לנמוך ויותר משבע אין. היינו למשל כשהולך ועולה במדריגות קול הנגינה מנמוך לגבוה, אזי מאחת ועד שבע הם קולות משונין דא מדא כל קול שמגביה הוא מין אחר לגמרי. וכשבא לקול דרגא השמינית הגבוה מכולם, הוא עצם וגוון חד עם קול הדרגא הראשונה הנמוכה מכולם שהתחיל בה, ואין הפרש ביניהם כלל אלא שהם אוקטובות חלוקים, זו אוקטובה גבוה וזו אוקכובה נמוכה. וכן היפוך כשהולך ויורד במדריגת קול הנגינה מגבוה לנמוך.

I s it known to musicians that all music is essentially built on a seven-tiered structure, namely, there are seven notes on an ascending scale and not more.

For example, when one ascends a note, from one note to the next—up to seven notes—each note is completely different from the other. But when one reaches the eighth note, it is essentially the same sound as the first note of the previous set; the only difference between them is that they are in different octaves—the present one being a higher octave than the previous. The same is also true when descending in musical notes.

TEXT 16B

Ibid.

כל מיני הקולות הנמצאים בעולם מחכמת נגינה והמוסיקה ומכל העולם הם כלולים משבע מדרגות הקול לא יותר, אלא שהם אוקטבות חלוקים גבוה על גבוה עד אין מספר, והיינו כנגד ז' קלין עילאין היינו ז' ימי הבנין הלא המה שבע מדות הקדושים מחסד ולמטה שיש בהם השגה בעולם הזה.

E very sound that exists on this earth, musical or of any type, falls somewhere on the scale of these seven notes, and not more, on different octaves without end. These seven notes correspond to the seven supernal sounds which are the seven days of Creation—the seven Divine Attributes from chesed and on, through which the world operates.

Pen of the Soul

TEXT 17

Rabbi Shmuel Zalmanov, Introduction to Sefer Hanigunim

What Chabad did to Chasidut in general occurred with the Chasidic song as well: Whereas the Baal Shem Tov injected a spirit of life into music, the Alter Rebbe of Chabad arrived and revealed the true depth and soul of the Chasidic song, known as a "niggun"...

The Chabad niggun appeared around the same time the Chabad philosophy was revealed, around the year 1772-1773. The Alter Rebbe, the founder of Chabad, was himself an accomplished musician and heartfelt composer of first-class caliber. He composed ten songs, deeply revered among the Chasidim, the most famous one being the "Song of Four Stanzas."

TEXT 18A

Rabbi Yosef Yitzchak Schneersohn of Lubavitch,
Sefer Hasichot 5702 p. 121-122

Rabbi Yosef Yitschak Schneersohn
(Rayats, Frierdiker Rebbe, Previous Rebbe)
1880–1950
Chasidic rebbe, prolific writer, and Jewish activist. Rabbi Yosef Yitschak, the 6th leader of the Chabad movement, actively promoted Jewish religious practice in Soviet Russia and was arrested for these activities. After his release from prison and exile, he settled in Warsaw, Poland, from where he fled Nazi occupation, and arrived in New York in 1940. Settling in Brooklyn, Rabbi Schneersohn worked to revitalize American Jewish life. His son-in law, Rabbi Menachem Mendel Schneerson, succeeded him as the leader of the Chabad movement.

Song and music is one of the practices and methods of Divine service that the Chasidim have as a tradition from the Baal Shem Tov…

The Alter Rebbe was once invited to deliver a Torah discourse at a wedding in Vitebsk. The Alter Rebbe delivered a sharp and brilliant discourse, comprised of advanced logic—all delivered as he spoke very quickly. The audience was very impressed and the Alter Rebbe said that "the tongue is the pen of the heart."

The audience then requested that the Alter Rebbe sing a song, for when the Alter Rebbe learned or prayed they would not be able to tear themselves away from the sweetness of his singing. The Alter Rebbe obliged and sang a niggun and he then said, "The tongue is the pen of the heart, and song is the pen of the soul."

TEXT 18B

Rabbi Dovber of Lubavitch
(Mitteler Rebbe)
1773–1827

Rabbi Dovber was the eldest son of and successor to Rabbi Shneur Zalman of Liadi and greatly expanded upon and developed his father's groundbreaking teachings. He was the first Chabad rebbe to live in the village of Lubavitch. Dedicated to the welfare of Russian Jewry, at that time confined to the Pale of Settlement, he established Jewish agricultural colonies. His most notable works on Chasidic thought include *Sha'ar Hayichud*, *Torat Chayim*, and *Imrei Binah*.

Rabbi DovBer Shneuri of Lubavitch, Sha'ar Hateshuvah 89a

וביאור הדבר הנה יש להקדים תחלה בשרש ענין הניגון בהיות שאנו רואים בחוש בכל ניגון שעיקרו ושרשו מגיע בעצם הנפש דוקא שהוא בחינת יחידה שבה השורה בבחינת נקודה פנימיות שבעומק הלב שלמעלה מן השכל לגמרי.

והמופת על זה כאשר אדם מנגן בכלי שיר באופנים שונים המורים השכלות מופלאות... הנה ודאי אותו המכוון בעומק ההשגה הנפלאה אשר לא יוכל לגלותו כלל בדיבור בפה לזולתו הוא מביא לידי גילוי אותו אור עומק המכוון הזה בניגון זה. ולא עוד אלא גם מה שלא השיג עדיין בכלי השכל שבמוחו לעוצם עומקו והעלמו הנפלאה הימנו... כי הרי לא יוכל עדיין להסביר לזולתו כלל, רק בשעה שמנגן נדמה לו כאלו משיג היטיב לעומק המכוון. וכן בבחינת שירה שבפה כשהוא מנגן בפיו, מפני שיוצא מנקודת לבבו מבחינת יחידה ששורה שם כנ"ל על כן גם בשכל הנפלא הימנו יכוין לעומק כאילו משיגו ממש.

We find that song has the power to reach the essence of the soul, namely the yechidah of the soul; a deep-seated point that completely transcends logic.

This is demonstrated by the fact that when one plays music with various instruments that display profound wisdom and art... The true depth of his intellectual grasp, that which cannot be expressed verbally to another, finds expression in the music. What's more, even with regards to the profundity that the person has not himself yet grasped due to its depth and abstractness... that he cannot explain to another whatsoever, when he plays music—he feels as if he truly understands it. The same is true when singing vocally.

The reason for this is because the music stems from the essence of his soul where the yechidah lies; thus, it enables the person to perceive wisdoms that are otherwise completely beyond him.

TEXT 18C

Ibid 98b

וגם אנו רואים בחוש ששרש הניגון למעלה גם מן הרצון והתענוג שנמשך מעצמות הנפש שהרי כל דאגה וצער היפך העונג יבטל השיר וגם כל עונג יבוטל לגבי עונג שבשיר כידוע המופת על זה מדבר והיפוכו שיש בשיר חדוה ומרירות שגם אם יהיה האדם בהתפעלות תענוג וחדוה בלתי מוגבל כאשר ישיר שיר של עוצב בקול ערב היוצא מנקודת הלב או בכלי שיר טוב יבוטל החדוה והעונג ויפול לבו בעוצב וצער עד שיבכה וכן להיפך אם האדם בצער ועוצב גדול כשישמע קול שיר של חדוה ועונג יתפעל בחדוה ותענוג עד שירקד כו'.

ומזה נראה שהעונג והצער שבכלי שיר למעלה מעונג וצער שבנפש עד אשר מושלים בהם כרצונם להפוך מצער שבנפש לתענוג ומתענוג לצער כו' אין זה רק מטעם ששרש הניגון מגיע בעצם הנפש שנקרא יחידה ששם בחי' העונג והצער בחינת מקור עצמי ולא בחינת התפשטות הארה לבד כידוע.

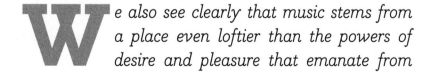

e also see clearly that music stems from a place even loftier than the powers of desire and pleasure that emanate from the essence of the soul, for any feeling of trouble or concern can be dispelled by music, and music can overpower any other pleasure as well.

We can see this power of music in everyday life: One may be in a state of tremendous pleasure and joy, but should he sing a melancholy song from the depths of his heart with a sweet voice, or listen to one being played well, the pleasure will dissipate and he will descend into melancholy to the point of tears.

The same is true for the opposite: A person can be extremely pained and depressed, but when he hears a pleasurable and joyous tune, he cannot help but be gladdened to the point of dancing.

This demonstrates that the powers of pleasure and pain contained within music are deeper than the pleasure and pain in the soul, to the extent that they can control the soul. The reason for this is because music stems from the essence of the soul called the yechidah, where pleasure and pain are in their most abstract and inherent state, not only an emanation thereof.

8

BEHA'ALOTECHA

Stand Up and Fight

Why Orthodoxy Is Not Complacency

Student Manual

PARSHA OVERVIEW
Beha'alotecha

Aaron is commanded to raise light in the lamps of the menorah, and the tribe of Levi initiated into the service in the Sanctuary.

A "Second Passover" is instituted in response to the petition "Why should we be deprived?" by a group of Jews who were unable to bring the Passover offering in its appointed time because they were ritually impure. G-d instructs Moses on the procedures for Israel's journeys andencampments in the desert, and the people journey in formation from Mount Sinai, where they had been camped for nearly a year.

The people are dissatisfied with their "bread from heaven" (the manna), and demand that Moses supply them with meat. Moses appoints 70 elders, to whom he imparts of his spirit, to assist him in the burden of governing the people. Miriam speaks negatively of Moses, and is punished with leprosy; Moses prays for her healing, and the entire community waits seven days for her recovery.

1. Why Should we Lose Out?

Pesach Sheini

TEXT 1A

Bamidbar 9:1-5

וַיְדַבֵּר ה' אֶל מֹשֶׁה בְמִדְבַּר סִינַי בַּשָּׁנָה הַשֵּׁנִית לְצֵאתָם מֵאֶרֶץ מִצְרַיִם בַּחֹדֶשׁ הָרִאשׁוֹן לֵאמֹר:

וְיַעֲשׂוּ בְנֵי יִשְׂרָאֵל אֶת הַפָּסַח בְּמוֹעֲדוֹ:

בְּאַרְבָּעָה עָשָׂר יוֹם בַּחֹדֶשׁ הַזֶּה בֵּין הָעַרְבַּיִם תַּעֲשׂוּ אֹתוֹ בְּמוֹעֲדוֹ כְּכָל חֻקֹּתָיו וּכְכָל מִשְׁפָּטָיו תַּעֲשׂוּ אֹתוֹ:

וַיְדַבֵּר מֹשֶׁה אֶל בְּנֵי יִשְׂרָאֵל לַעֲשֹׂת הַפָּסַח:

וַיַּעֲשׂוּ אֶת הַפֶּסַח בָּרִאשׁוֹן בְּאַרְבָּעָה עָשָׂר יוֹם לַחֹדֶשׁ בֵּין הָעַרְבַּיִם בְּמִדְבַּר סִינַי כְּכֹל אֲשֶׁר צִוָּה ה' אֶת מֹשֶׁה כֵּן עָשׂוּ בְּנֵי יִשְׂרָאֵל:

G-d spoke to Moses in the Sinai Desert, in the second year of their exodus from the land of Egypt, in the first month, saying:

"The children of Israel shall make the Passover sacrifice in its appointed time.

"On the afternoon of the fourteenth of this month, you shall make it in its appointed time; in accordance with all its statutes and all its ordinances you shall make it."

Moses spoke to the children of Israel [instructing them] to make the Passover sacrifice.

So they made the Passover sacrifice in the first month, on the afternoon of the fourteenth day of the month in the Sinai Desert; according to all that G-d had commanded Moses, so did the children of Israel do.

TEXT 1B

Ibid. 9:6-8

וַיְהִי אֲנָשִׁים אֲשֶׁר הָיוּ טְמֵאִים לְנֶפֶשׁ אָדָם וְלֹא יָכְלוּ לַעֲשֹׂת הַפֶּסַח בַּיּוֹם הַהוּא וַיִּקְרְבוּ לִפְנֵי מֹשֶׁה וְלִפְנֵי אַהֲרֹן בַּיּוֹם הַהוּא:

וַיֹּאמְרוּ הָאֲנָשִׁים הָהֵמָּה אֵלָיו אֲנַחְנוּ טְמֵאִים לְנֶפֶשׁ אָדָם לָמָּה נִגָּרַע לְבִלְתִּי הַקְרִב אֶת קָרְבַּן ה' בְּמֹעֲדוֹ בְּתוֹךְ בְּנֵי יִשְׂרָאֵל:

וַיֹּאמֶר אֲלֵהֶם מֹשֶׁה עִמְדוּ וְאֶשְׁמְעָה מַה יְצַוֶּה ה' לָכֶם:

There were men who were ritually unclean [because of contact] with a dead person, and therefore could not make the Passover sacrifice on that day. So they approached Moses and Aaron on that day.

Those men said to him, "We are ritually unclean [because of contact] with a dead person; [but] why should we be excluded so as not to bring the offering of G-d in its appointed time, with all the children of Israel?"

Moses said to them, "Wait, and I will hear what G-d instructs concerning you."

TEXT 1C

Ibid. 9:9-14

וַיְדַבֵּר ה׳ אֶל מֹשֶׁה לֵּאמֹר:

דַּבֵּר אֶל בְּנֵי יִשְׂרָאֵל לֵאמֹר אִישׁ אִישׁ כִּי יִהְיֶה טָמֵא לָנֶפֶשׁ אוֹ בְדֶרֶךְ רְחֹקָה לָכֶם אוֹ לְדֹרֹתֵיכֶם וְעָשָׂה פֶסַח לַה׳:

בַּחֹדֶשׁ הַשֵּׁנִי בְּאַרְבָּעָה עָשָׂר יוֹם בֵּין הָעַרְבַּיִם יַעֲשׂוּ אֹתוֹ עַל מַצּוֹת וּמְרֹרִים יֹאכְלֻהוּ:

לֹא יַשְׁאִירוּ מִמֶּנּוּ עַד בֹּקֶר וְעֶצֶם לֹא יִשְׁבְּרוּ בוֹ כְּכָל חֻקַּת הַפֶּסַח יַעֲשׂוּ אֹתוֹ:

וְהָאִישׁ אֲשֶׁר הוּא טָהוֹר וּבְדֶרֶךְ לֹא הָיָה וְחָדַל לַעֲשׂוֹת הַפֶּסַח וְנִכְרְתָה הַנֶּפֶשׁ הַהִוא מֵעַמֶּיהָ כִּי קָרְבַּן ה׳ לֹא הִקְרִיב בְּמֹעֲדוֹ חֶטְאוֹ יִשָּׂא הָאִישׁ הַהוּא:

וְכִי יָגוּר אִתְּכֶם גֵּר וְעָשָׂה פֶסַח לַה׳ כְּחֻקַּת הַפֶּסַח וּכְמִשְׁפָּטוֹ כֵּן יַעֲשֶׂה חֻקָּה אַחַת יִהְיֶה לָכֶם וְלַגֵּר וּלְאֶזְרַח הָאָרֶץ:

G-d spoke to Moses saying:

Speak to the children of Israel saying, "Any person who becomes unclean from [contact with] the dead, or is on a distant journey, whether among you or in future generations, he shall make a Passover sacrifice for G-d.

"In the second month, on the fourteenth day, in the afternoon, they shall make it; they shall eat it with unleavened cakes and bitter herbs.

"They shall not leave over anything from it until the next morning, and they shall not break any of its bones. They shall make it in accordance with all the statutes connected with the Passover sacrifice.

"But the man who was ritually clean and was not on a journey, yet refrained from making the Passover sacrifice, his soul shall be cut off from his people, for he did not bring the offering of G-d in its appointed time; that person shall bear his sin.

"If a proselyte dwells with you, and he makes a Passover sacrifice to G-d, according to the statutes of the Passover sacrifice and its ordinances he shall make it. One statute shall apply to you, to the proselyte, and to the native-born citizen."

Question—Funny Claim

TEXT 2

Rabbi Shlomo Ephraim ben Aharon of Luntshits, Keli Yakar ad loc.

יש מקשים וכי נעלם מהם שטמא אסור באכילת קדשים?

Many ask: Did they forget that one who is ritually impure is not allowed to partake of the sacrifices?

Rabbi Shlomo Ephraim ben Aharon of Luntshits
1550–1619
After studying in the yeshivah of the Maharshal, Rabbi Shlomo Ephraim gained a reputation as a distinguished preacher and scholar. He traveled far and wide to deliver his fiery sermons, which were collected and published. He is primarily known today for his work *Keli Yakar*, and for his commentary on the Pentateuch, which was subsequently printed in many editions of the Bible.

Nice Guys Finish Last

TEXT 3

Babylonian Talmud
A literary work of monumental proportions that draws upon the legal, spiritual, intellectual, ethical, and historical traditions of Judaism. The 37 tractates of the Babylonian Talmud contain the teachings of the Jewish sages from the period after the destruction of the 2nd Temple through the 5th century CE. It has served as the primary vehicle for the transmission of the Oral Law and the education of Jews over the centuries; it is the entry point for all subsequent legal, ethical, and theological Jewish scholarship.

Talmud Tractate Sukkah 25a-b

ויהי אנשים אשר היו טמאים לנפש אדם וכו' אותם אנשים מי היו? נושאי ארונו של יוסף היו, דברי רבי יוסי הגלילי. רבי עקיבא אומר: מישאל ואלצפן היו שהיו עוסקין בנדב ואביהוא. ר' יצחק אומר... עוסקין במת מצוה היו שחל שביעי שלהן להיות בערב פסח.

"*There were men who were ritually unclean [because of contact] with a dead person, etc." Who were these men? They were those who bore the coffin of Joseph. So said Rabbi Yose the Galilean.*

Rabbi Akiva said: they were Mishael and Elzaphan who handled [the remains of] Nadav and Avihu. Rabbi Yitzchak said... they were involved with an unknown corpse (met mitzvah) and their seventh day of impurity was the day before Pesach.

TEXT 4

Maimonides, Mishneh Torah Laws of the Paschal Lamb 7:1

רבים שהיו טמאי מת בפסח ראשון אם היו מיעוט הקהל הרי אלו נדחין
לפסח שני כשאר הטמאים אבל אם היו רוב הקהל טמאי מת או שהיו
הכהנים או כלי שרת טמאים טומאת מת אינן נדחין, אלא יקריבו כולן
הפסח בטומאה הטמאים עם טהורים.

When many individuals were ritually impure due to contact with a human corpse on the first Pesach:

If they were the lesser portion of the Jewish people, their offering is postponed to the second Pesach like other impure individuals. If, however, the majority of the Jewish people were impure due to contact with a human corpse, or the priests or the sacred utensils were impure due to contact with a human corpse, their offering is not postponed. Instead, they should all offer the Paschal sacrifice in a state of ritual impurity, those ritually impure together with those who are pure.

Rabbi Moshe ben Maimon
(Maimonides, Rambam)
1135–1204

Halachist, philosopher, author, and physician. Maimonides was born in Cordoba, Spain. After the conquest of Cordoba by the Almohads, he fled Spain and eventually settled in Cairo, Egypt. There, he became the leader of the Jewish community and served as court physician to the vizier of Egypt. He is most noted for authoring the *Mishneh Torah*, an encyclopedic arrangement of Jewish law, and for his philosophical work, *Guide for the Perplexed*.

TEXT 5

Rabbi Chayim ibn Atar
(Or Hachayim)
1696–1743

Biblical exegete, Kabbalist, and Talmudist. Rabbi Atar, born in Meknes, Morocco, was a prominent member of the Moroccan rabbinate and later immigrated to the Land of Israel. He is most famous for his *Or Hachayim*, a popular commentary on the Torah. The famed Jewish historian and bibliophile Rabbi Chaim Yosef David Azulai was among his most notable disciples.

Rabbi Chayim ibn Atar, Ohr Hachaim Bamidbar ad loc.

ואולי כי לצד שנטמאו ברשותו יתברך, בין למאן דאמר טמאי מת מצוה, בין למאן דאמר נושאי ארונו של יוסף, חשבו כי ידין ה' אותם כטהורים, וכשם שמצינו שיתרצה ה' עשות הפסח בטומאה בציבור, לזה טענו למה נגרע, וכי בשביל שעשו מצוה יהיו נגרעים מקרבן פסח.

According to both opinions mentioned in the Talmud (if it was Yosef's coffin bearers or people who were impure because of a met mitzvah), these people contracted impurity in accordance with G-d's will. They therefore thought that G-d would consider them pure, just as we find that G-d wishes that the Paschal lamb be offered when the entire community is impure. For this reason, they claimed, "Why should we be excluded?" i.e., "just because we did a mitzvah means we should be excluded from the Paschal lamb?!"

2. Give and Take

On the Receiving End

TEXT 6

Talmud Tractate Shabbat 88a

אמר רבי אלעזר: בשעה שהקדימו ישראל נעשה לנשמע יצתה בת קול ואמרה להן: מי גילה לבני רז זה שמלאכי השרת משתמשין בו? דכתיב "ברכו ה' מלאכיו גברי כח עשי דברו לשמע בקול דברו", ברישא עשי, והדר לשמע. (מוכנין לעשות קודם שישמעו, ולא כדרך שאר עבדים ששומעים תחילה את הדבר, לידע אם יכולין לקבלן עליהם אם לאו. –רש"י)

Rabbi Elazar said: When the Jews proclaimed "we will do" before "we will listen," a Heavenly Voice went forth and exclaimed to them, "Who revealed to My children this secret, which is employed by the Ministering Angels, as it is written, 'Bless G-d, angels of his. Mighty in strength, that fulfill his word, that hearken unto the voice of his word.' First they fulfill and then they hearken!"

(They are ready to fulfill before they listen, unlike most other servants who first hear out the instructions and gauge whether or not they are able to fulfill it. –Rashi)

Born to Contribute

TEXT 7

Midrash Tanchuma Shemot §9

אמר דוד לפני הקדוש ברוך הוא רבון העולם "ישב עולם לפני אלקים"
תיישר עולמך בשוה העשירים והעניים, אמר ליה אם כן חסד ואמת מן
ינצרוהו, אם יהיו כולם עשירים או עניים מי יוכל לעשות חסד?

King David said to G-d, "Master of the universe, 'May he dwell forever [literally "may the world be settled"] before G-d!' —make your world equal, no man rich or poor!"

G-d responded, "If so, 'kindness and truth who will guard?' If all are rich or all are poor, who would be able to bestow kindness?"

TEXT 8A

The Lubavitcher Rebbe, Torat Menachem 5744 vol. 3 p. 1677

הקדוש ברוך הוא ברא את העולם באופן כזה שכל נברא הוא גם
"מקבל" וגם "משפיע"... כי אפילו דבר קטן שבקטנים (מצד מעלתו)
יש בו מעלה מסויימת שאינה בכל שאר עניני העולם, וביחס למעלה
זו—הרי הוא בבחינת "משפיע" בכל שאר הענינים שבעולם (שכולם
"מקבלים" ממנו), ועד שפרט זה משלים את הבריאה כולה.

Tanchuma

A Midrashic work bearing the name of Rabbi Tanchuma, a 4th-century Talmudic sage quoted often in this work. This Midrash provides textual exegeses and stories, expounds upon the biblical narrative, and develops and illustrates moral principles. *Tanchuma* is unique in that many of its sections commence with a halachic discussion, which subsequently leads into non-halachic teachings.

G-d created the world in such a manner that every creature functions as both a "recipient" as well as a "contributor."… Even the smallest thing (in stature) possesses a certain quality that no other creature on earth has. With regards to that quality, it "contributes" to the entire world, to the extent that it can be said that this one detail completes the entire creation.

Rabbi Menachem Mendel Schneerson
1902–1994
The towering Jewish leader of the 20th century, known as "the Lubavitcher Rebbe," or simply as "the Rebbe." Born in southern Ukraine, the Rebbe escaped Nazi occupied Europe, arriving in the U.S. in June 1941. The Rebbe inspired and guided the revival of traditional Judaism after the European devastation, impacting virtually every Jewish community the world over. The Rebbe often emphasized that the performance of just one additional good deed could usher in the era of Mashiach. The Rebbe's scholarly talks and writings have been printed in more than 200 volumes.

TEXT 8B

Ibid. 3 p. 1677

בכל דבר שברא הקדוש ברוך הוא בעולמו (גם הדבר היותר תחתון) יש מעלה מיוחדת שאינה בשאר כל הדברים, ומצד מעלה זו נעשה הוא בבחינת "משפיע" לשאר הדברים שלמעלה ממנו, שהם מקבלים ממנו את המעלה שישנה בו. וזה כלל בכל דבר שבקדושה—שצריך להיות בו ענין ההשפעה.

Anything that G-d created in this world (even the lowliest of matter) possesses a certain quality that cannot be found anywhere else. Regarding this quality, the creature becomes a "contributor" to the rest of the world—even things of higher stature. This is a general rule when it comes to matters of holiness—it must have a contributing element.

TEXT 9

Rabbi Shneur Zalman of Liadi (Alter Rebbe) 1745–1812

Chasidic rebbe, halachic authority, and founder of the Chabad movement. The Alter Rebbe was born in Liozna, Belarus, and was among the principal students of the Magid of Mezeritch. His numerous works include the *Tanya*, an early classic containing the fundamentals of Chabad Chasidism, and *Shulchan Aruch HaRav*, a code of Jewish law.

Rabbi Shneur Zalman of Liadi, Tanya ch. 24

יתוש שמכניס ואינו מוציא שהיא קליפה היותר תחתונה ורחוקה מבחינת הקדושה המשפעת בתכלית הריחוק.

The mosquito—which consumes but does not excrete, is the lowest of negative forces and the most distant from holiness, which bestows benevolence even at the greatest distance.

TEXT 10

Torah Menachem Ibid. p. 1677

וזאת—כדי שלא יהיה ענין של נפילת-רוח או נמיכות-רוח אצל אף נברא שבעולם.

The reason for this is so that no creature in the world should ever experience a feeling of depression or downtrodden spirit.

3. It's up to Us

Designed to Fix

TEXT 11

Midrash Bereishit Rabah 11:6

פילוסופוס אחד שאל את רבי הושעיה, אמר לו אם חביבה היא המילה מפני מה לא נתנה לאדם הראשון?

אמר לו מפני מה אותו האיש מגלח פאת ראשו, ומניח את פאת זקנו?

אמר לו מפני מה שגדל עמו בשטות.

אמר לו אם כן יסמא את עינו ויקטע את ידיו וישבר את רגליו על ידי שגדלו עמו בשטות.

אמר לו ולאלין מיליא אתינן, אתמהא?

אמר לו להוציאך חלק אי אפשר, אלא כל מה שנברא בששת ימי בראשית צריכין עשייה, כגון החרדל צריך למתוק, התורמוסים צריך למתוק, החיטין צריכין להטחן, אפילו אדם צריך תיקון.

Bereishit Rabah

An early rabbinic commentary on the Book of Genesis. This Midrash bears the name of Rabbi Oshiya Rabah (Rabbi Oshiya "the Great") whose teaching opens this work. This Midrash provides textual exegeses and stories, expounds upon the biblical narrative, and develops and illustrates moral principles. Produced by the sages of the Talmud in the Land of Israel, its use of Aramaic closely resembles that of the Jerusalem Talmud. It was first published in Constantinople in 1512 together with four other Midrashic works on the other four books of the Pentateuch.

A philosopher once asked Rabbi Hoshaya, "If brit milah *is so dear to your G-d, why didn't He create Adam circumcised?"*

Rabbi Hoshaya responded, "Why do you shave your sideburns but not your beard?"

"The hair on my head grew in my [youthful years of] folly."

"If so, why don't you blind your eyes, cut your hands, and break your feet which also grew in your [youthful years of] folly?"

"Where is this conversation going?" asked the philosopher.

Rabbi Hoshaya responded, "You cannot do your part and answer my questions, [but I will answer yours]: Everything G-d created during the six days of creation requires some doing. Mustard needs to be sweetened; lupine [a bitter Mediterranean legume] needs to be sweetened; wheat requires grinding. Even man needs correction."

TEXT 12A

Talmud Tractate Shabbat 10a

כל דיין שדן דין אמת לאמיתו אפילו שעה אחת, מעלה עליו הכתוב כאילו נעשה שותף להקדוש ברוך הוא במעשה בראשית.

Every judge who judges with absolute integrity even for a single hour, Scripture gives him credit as though he had become a partner to the Holy One, blessed be He, in the creation.

TEXT 12B

Ibid. 119b

כל המתפלל בערב שבת ואומר ויכלו, מעלה עליו הכתוב כאילו נעשה שותף להקדוש ברוך הוא במעשה בראשית, שנאמר ויכלו, אל תקרי ויכלו אלא ויכלו.

H e who prays on the eve of the Shabbat and recites, "And [heaven and earth] were finished," Scripture treats of him as though he had become a partner with the Holy One, blessed be He, in the Creation, for it is said, "Vayechulu [and they were finished]"; read not "Vayechulu," but "Vayechalu [and they finished]."

In Torah and Mitzvot

TEXT 13A

Talmud Tractate Megillah 19b

ואמר רבי חייא בר אבא אמר רבי יוחנן: מאי דכתיב "ועליהם ככל הדברים אשר דבר ה' עמכם בהר". מלמד שהראהו הקדוש ברוך הוא למשה דקדוקי תורה ודקדוקי סופרים, ומה שהסופרים עתידין לחדש.

R abbi Chiya bar Abba said in the name of Rabbi Yochanan: What is the meaning of the verse, "And on them [the tablets] was written according to all the words which G-d spoke with you in the mount"? It teaches us that the Holy One, blessed *be He, showed Moses the minutiae of the Torah, and the minutiae of the Sages, and the innovations which would be introduced by the Sages.*

TEXT 13B

Pirkei Avot
(Ethics of the Fathers)

A 6-chapter work on Jewish ethics that is studied widely by Jewish communities, especially during the summer. The first 5 chapters are from the Mishnah, tractate Avot. Avot differs from the rest of the Mishnah in that it does not focus on legal subjects; it is a collection of the sages' wisdom on topics related to character development, ethics, healthy living, piety, and the study of Torah.

Mishnah Avot 5:20

יהי רצון מלפניך ה' אלקינו שיבנה בית המקדש במהרה בימינו ותן חלקנו בתורתך.

May it be the will [emanating] from Your presence, o Lord our G-d, that Your city be [re]built speedily in our days and grant us our portion in Your law.

The Pesach Sheini Initiative

TEXT 14A

The Lubavitcher Rebbe, Torat Menachem ibid. p. 1680-1

וביותר מודגש זה בציווי פסח שני—שכל עיקרו לא בא אלא על ידי פעולתן של ישראל, שתבעו אצל משה רבינו: "למה נגרע". וכאשר משה רבינו הביא את תביעתן לפני הקדוש ברוך הוא, נותן התורה ומצוה המצוות—אזי נתחדש הציווי דפסח שני.

ומזה יש ללמוד הוראה נפלאה בעבודת ה'. ובהקדים:

לכאורה, תביעתם של האנשים שלא יכלו להקריב קרבן פסח במועדו, "למה נגרע"—תמוהה ביותר... אלא מכאן למדים אנו הוראה נפלאה—שכאשר יהודי מרגיש שחסר לו משהו בענין הקשור עם יראת-שמים, תורה ומצוותיה, אינו סומך על אף אחד, לא על משה רבנו ואפילו לא על הקדוש ברוך הוא (כביכול), ואינו אומר "אין לנו להשען אלא על אבינו שבשמים..."—אלא צועק ותובע: "למה נגרע"!

כאשר מדובר אודות עניני יראת-שמים — אומרת תורה "הכל בידי שמים חוץ מיראת שמים" ולכן, רצונו של הקדוש ברוך הוא שיהודי יתבע וידרוש בהתאם להרגש שלו בעניני יראת-שמים, וכאשר מראה את גודל תשוקתו וחפצו—ממלא הקדוש ברוך הוא את רצונו, כפי שרואים בנוגע לפסח שני, שבעקבות הטענה "למה נגרע", נתחדש ציווי בתורה.

The mitzvah of Pesach Sheini *highlights this idea. In its entirety, this mitzvah only came about due to the initiative of the Jews who demanded from Moses, "Why should we be excluded?!" When Moses brought their demands before G-d—the Giver of Torah and Instructor of* mitzvot*—the mitzvah of* Pesach Sheini *was born.*

We can derive a phenomenal lesson from this in our Divine service.

At face value, the demand of these people who couldn't offer the Paschal lamb at the right time, "Why should we be excluded" is incomprehensible... [In truth,] it teaches us a marvelous message: When a Jew feels that he is lacking something in relation to his Fear of Heaven, Torah, mitzvot *et al., he is not to rely on*

anyone; not on Moses, and not even on G-d Himself
(so to speak) and throw around epithets such as "Upon
whom is it for us to rely? Only upon our Father who
is in Heaven!" Rather, he should [take matters into his
own hands and] scream and demand, "Why should
we be excluded?!"

When speaking of matters pertaining to fear of Heaven,
the Torah declares that, "All is in the hands of Heaven
except for the fear of Heaven!" As such, G-d wishes
that a Jew should demand and search as befits his own
personal feelings regarding fearing Heaven. When he
demonstrates a true desire and passion, G-d fulfills
his request, as we see regarding Pesach Sheini—as a
result of the demand, "Why should we be excluded," a
new mitzvah was born. ·

TEXT 14B

Ibid. p. 1681-3

ההוראה ליהודי פשוט שבפשוטים:

כאשר מתבונן במעמדו ומצבו ויודע ומכיר בכך **שהוא פשוט
שבפשוטים**—יכול לחשוב: מי אני ומה אני לבוא בתביעה כו', ומה אוכל
כבר לפעול!?

הנה על זה באה ההוראה מפסח שני:...

**באו יהודים בתביעה ודרישה להקדוש ברוך הוא "למה נגרע", ולא עוד
אלא שתביעתם ודרישתם אכן נתקבלה, וניתן להם הציווי דפסח שני**...

יהודי צריך לדעת את הכחות שיש בידו... עליו לדעת שבעניינים הקשורים עם יראת-שמים, ממתין הקדוש ברוך הוא שיהודי יראה שהדבר נוגע לו, ולא רק בפנימיות נפשו, אלא גם בכחות הנפש, במחשבה ובדיבורו, עד לענין של מעשה, ואז—מקבלים את תביעתו ודרישתו, ועד כדי כך שעל ידו מתחדש ענין בתורה הפועל שלימות בכללות הענין דתורה ומצות עבור כל בני ישראל.

T he lesson for even the simplest Jew:

When a Jew thinks about his standing and recognizes that he is exceedingly simple, it can lead to thoughts such as, "Who am I to demand anything? What can I possibly accomplish?"

The lesson from Pesach Sheini comes and tells us:...

A group of Jews approached G-d with a demand, "Why should we be excluded?—and their demand was granted, bestowing upon them the mitzvah of Pesach Sheini...

A Jew must be cognizant of the power he possesses... he must be aware that when it comes to matters concerning fear of Heaven, G-d is waiting for the Jew to take matters to heart, and not only subconsciously, but in an explicit manner, through expressing it in thought, speech, and even action. Then, his demands are met, to the extent that he will contribute a novel item to Torah, effectively "bettering" the whole of Judaism for the entire Jewish people.

Demanding Mashiach

TEXT 14C

Ibid.

ישנם הטוענים: מדוע מדברים ומכריזים ללא הרף על הנושא של ביאת המשיח, "אני מאמין.. בביאת המשיח .. אחכה לו בכל יום שיבוא"—יש לסמוך על הקדוש ברוך הוא שיגאל את ישראל מתי שירצה?! הקדוש ברוך הוא הוא שלח את בני שראל לגלות, והוא זה שצריך לגאול אותם! הנה על זה בא הלימוד וההוראה מ"פסח שני":

לכאורה, היתה מצוה זו צריכה להנתן על ידי הקדוש ברוך הוא בעצמו— ככל שאר רמ"ז מצוות עשה. ואף על פי כן רואים שכל עיקרה של מצוה זו... נפעל—כאמור—על ידי הדרישה והתביעה של ישראל, שלא סמכו על הקדוש ברוך הוא (כביכול)... אלא תבעו שרצונם להקריב קרבן פסח, ועל ידי זה פעלו שיתחדש ציווי בתורה...

ועל דרך זה בעניננו—בקשת ותביעת בני ישראל אודות הגאולה: לא זו בלבד שבקשה ותביעה זו אינה היפך התורה חס ושלום, אלא אדרבה—התורה ציוותה להתנהג כן, על ידי אנשי כנסת הגדולה, שתיקנו שכאשר יהודי מבקש צרכיו מהקדוש ברוך הוא בעת תפלת העמידה—יאמר בתפלתו: "את צמח דוד עבדך מהרה תצמיח... כי לישועתך קוינו כל היום", "ותחזינה עינינו בשובך לציון"! ואינו מסתפק בכך שמבקש ודורש זאת בתפלה אחת—אלא חוזר על בקשה ותביעה זו בכל תפלה ותפלה, ג' פעמים ככל יום!... בני ישראל מבקשים וצועקים—ביחד עם דוד המלך, דוד מלכא משיחא, "עד מתי"...

There are those who question: *Why do we speak so incessantly about the topic of Mashiach's arrival, "I believe... in the coming of Mashiach... I await his coming every day"—why not just rely on G-d to redeem the Jewish people when-ever He so wishes?! G-d sent the Jews into exile, and He'll redeem them!*

It is regarding this that the lesson of Pesach Sheini *comes in:*

It would seem appropriate that this mitzvah be given by G-d Himself like the other 247 positive mitzvot in the Torah. Yet, we find that the mitzvah only came about..., as mentioned, as a result of the demands of the Jews who did not rely on G-d (so to speak)... They demanded that they want to offer the Paschal lamb, and thus caused that a new mitzvah be established...

The same is true with regards to the topic of demanding the redemption:

Not only are such demands not contradictory to Torah, but on the contrary—the Torah instructs us to do so, in the form of the Men of the Great Assembly who decreed that when a Jew demands his needs in prayer, he should say, "Speedily cause the scion of David Your servant to flourish... for we hope for Your salvation all day... May our eyes behold Your return to Zion."

A Jew is not satisfied with making this request once a day, and repeats this request in each prayer, three times every day!...

The Jewish people request and cry out, together with King David, the King Mashiach, "Ad Masai?! Till when [will we languish in exile]?!"

TEXT 14D

Ibid.

ישנו פסק דין ברור ברמב״ם ״שיהא אדם… שואל צרכיו שהוא צריך להם״, היינו, שכאשר יהודי מרגיש שחסר לו משהו—עליו לבקש על זה מהקדוש ברוך הוא בכל עת מצוא. ועל פי זה: אם בנוגע ל״מזוני״ מבקש האדם מהקדוש ברוך הוא שיתן לו ״מזוני רויחי״… הרי על אחת כמה וכמה כאשר מדובר אודות ענין הגאולה—הנה למרות היותו בטוח שהגאולה תבוא, אינו יכול להשאר אדיש ולהמתין שהגאולה תבוא ״מחרתיים״, כאשר ביכלתו לפעול שתבוא מחר!

Maimonides explicitly rules, *"That a person… should request his needs from G-d every day,"* namely, that when a Jew feels that he lacks something, he is instructed to turn to G-d at any opportunity.

Accordingly: If a person can ask G-d to bestow upon him plentiful livelihood… it can certainly be so with regards to the redemption. Despite the fact that he is sure that the redemption will indeed happen, he is unable to remain indifferent and wait for it to happen the day after tomorrow if he can do something to make it happen tomorrow!

9

SHELACH

Crippling Insecurity

Never Doubt Yourself

Student Manual

PARSHA OVERVIEW
Shelach

Moses sends twelve spies to the land of Canaan. Forty days later they return, carrying a huge cluster of grapes, a pomegranate and a fig, to report on a lush and bountiful land. But ten of the spies warn that the inhabitants of the land are giants and warriors "more powerful than we"; only Caleb and Joshua insist that the land can be conquered, as G-d has commanded.

The people weep that they'd rather return to Egypt. G-d decrees that Israel's entry into the Land shall be delayed forty years, during which time that entire generation will die out in the desert. A group of remorseful Jews storm the mountain on the border of the Land, and are routed by the Amalekites and Canaanites.

The laws of the menachot (meal, wine and oil offerings) are given, as well as the mitzvah to consecrate a portion of the dough (challah) to G-d when making bread. A man violates the Shabbat by gathering sticks, and is put to death. G-d instructs to place fringes (tzitzit) on the four corners of our garments, so that we should remember to fulfill the mitzvot (divine commandments).

1. Frightful Report

The Spies' Report

TEXT 1A

Bamidbar (Numbers) 13:25-29, 31-33

וַיָּשֻׁבוּ מִתּוּר הָאָרֶץ מִקֵּץ אַרְבָּעִים יוֹם:

וַיֵּלְכוּ וַיָּבֹאוּ אֶל מֹשֶׁה וְאֶל אַהֲרֹן וְאֶל כָּל עֲדַת בְּנֵי יִשְׂרָאֵל אֶל מִדְבַּר פָּארָן

קָדֵשָׁה וַיָּשִׁיבוּ אוֹתָם דָּבָר וְאֶת כָּל הָעֵדָה וַיַּרְאוּם אֶת פְּרִי הָאָרֶץ:

וַיְסַפְּרוּ לוֹ וַיֹּאמְרוּ בָּאנוּ אֶל הָאָרֶץ אֲשֶׁר שְׁלַחְתָּנוּ וְגַם זָבַת חָלָב וּדְבַשׁ

הִוא וְזֶה פִּרְיָהּ:

אֶפֶס כִּי עַז הָעָם הַיֹּשֵׁב בָּאָרֶץ וְהֶעָרִים בְּצֻרוֹת גְּדֹלֹת מְאֹד וְגַם יַלְדֵי הָעֲנָק

רָאִינוּ שָׁם:

עֲמָלֵק יוֹשֵׁב בְּאֶרֶץ הַנֶּגֶב וְהַחִתִּי וְהַיְבוּסִי וְהָאֱמֹרִי יוֹשֵׁב בָּהָר וְהַכְּנַעֲנִי יֹשֵׁב

עַל הַיָּם וְעַל יַד הַיַּרְדֵּן:...

וְהָאֲנָשִׁים אֲשֶׁר עָלוּ עִמּוֹ אָמְרוּ לֹא נוּכַל לַעֲלוֹת אֶל הָעָם כִּי חָזָק הוּא מִמֶּנּוּ:

וַיֹּצִיאוּ דִּבַּת הָאָרֶץ אֲשֶׁר תָּרוּ אֹתָהּ אֶל בְּנֵי יִשְׂרָאֵל לֵאמֹר הָאָרֶץ אֲשֶׁר

עָבַרְנוּ בָהּ לָתוּר אֹתָהּ אֶרֶץ אֹכֶלֶת יוֹשְׁבֶיהָ הִוא וְכָל הָעָם אֲשֶׁר רָאִינוּ

בְּתוֹכָהּ אַנְשֵׁי מִדּוֹת:

וְשָׁם רָאִינוּ אֶת הַנְּפִילִים בְּנֵי עֲנָק מִן הַנְּפִלִים וַנְּהִי בְעֵינֵינוּ כַּחֲגָבִים וְכֵן

הָיִינוּ בְּעֵינֵיהֶם:

They returned from scouting the Land at the end of forty days.

They went, and they came to Moses and Aaron and all the congregation of the children of Israel in the desert of Paran, to Kadesh. They brought them

back a report, as well as to the entire congregation, and they showed them the fruit of the land.

They told him and said, "We came to the land to which you sent us, and it is flowing with milk and honey, and this is its fruit.

"However, the people who inhabit the land are mighty, and the cities are extremely huge and fortified, and there we saw even the offspring of the giant.

"The Amalekites dwell in the south land, while the Hittites, the Jebusites, and the Amorites dwell in the mountainous region. The Canaanites dwell on the coast and alongside the Jordan."…

But the men who went up with him said, "We are unable to go up against the people, for they are stronger than we."

They spread an [evil] report about the land which they had scouted, telling the children of Israel, "The land we passed through to explore is a land that consumes its inhabitants, and all the people we saw in it are men of stature.

"There we saw the giants, the sons of Anak, descended from the giants. In our eyes, we seemed like grasshoppers, and so we were in their eyes."

Question—They Weren't Wrong!

TEXT 2

Ibid. 14:42-43

אַל תַּעֲלוּ כִּי אֵין ה׳ בְּקִרְבְּכֶם וְלֹא תִּנָּגְפוּ לִפְנֵי אֹיְבֵיכֶם:
כִּי הָעֲמָלֵקִי וְהַכְּנַעֲנִי שָׁם לִפְנֵיכֶם וּנְפַלְתֶּם בֶּחָרֶב כִּי עַל כֵּן שַׁבְתֶּם מֵאַחֲרֵי
ה׳ וְלֹא יִהְיֶה ה׳ עִמָּכֶם:

Do not go up, for G-d is not among you, [so that] you will not be beaten by your enemies.

For the Amalekites and the Canaanites are there before you, and you will fall by the sword. For you have turned away from G-d, and G-d will not be with you.

Question—No Rebuttal

TEXT 3A

Ibid. 13:30

וַיַּהַס כָּלֵב אֶת הָעָם אֶל מֹשֶׁה וַיֹּאמֶר עָלֹה נַעֲלֶה וְיָרַשְׁנוּ אֹתָהּ כִּי יָכוֹל נוּכַל לָהּ:

Caleb silenced the people to [hear about] Moses, and he said, "We can surely go up and take possession of it, for we can indeed overcome it."

TEXT 3B

Ibid. 14:6-9

וִיהוֹשֻׁעַ בִּן נוּן וְכָלֵב בֶּן יְפֻנֶּה מִן הַתָּרִים אֶת הָאָרֶץ קָרְעוּ בִּגְדֵיהֶם:
וַיֹּאמְרוּ אֶל כָּל עֲדַת בְּנֵי יִשְׂרָאֵל לֵאמֹר הָאָרֶץ אֲשֶׁר עָבַרְנוּ בָהּ לָתוּר אֹתָהּ טוֹבָה הָאָרֶץ מְאֹד מְאֹד:
אִם חָפֵץ בָּנוּ ה' וְהֵבִיא אֹתָנוּ אֶל הָאָרֶץ הַזֹּאת וּנְתָנָהּ לָנוּ אֶרֶץ אֲשֶׁר הִוא זָבַת חָלָב וּדְבָשׁ:
אַךְ בַּה' אַל תִּמְרֹדוּ וְאַתֶּם אַל תִּירְאוּ אֶת עַם הָאָרֶץ כִּי לַחְמֵנוּ הֵם סָר צִלָּם מֵעֲלֵיהֶם וַה' אִתָּנוּ אַל תִּירָאֻם:

Joshua the son of Nun and Caleb the son of Yephuneh, who were among those who had scouted the land, tore their clothes.

They spoke to the entire congregation of the children of Israel, saying, "The land we passed through to scout is an exceedingly good land.

"If G-d desires us, He will bring us to this land and give it to us, a land flowing with milk and honey.

"But you shall not rebel against G-d, and you will not fear the people of that land for they are [as] our bread. Their protection is removed from them, and G-d is with us; do not fear them."

Heretical Conclusion

TEXT 4

Rabbi Moshe ben Nachman
(Nachmanides, Ramban)
1194–1270

Scholar, philosopher, author and physician. Nachmanides was born in Spain and served as leader of Iberian Jewry. In 1263, he was summoned by King James of Aragon to a public disputation with Pablo Cristiani, a Jewish apostate. Though Nachmanides was the clear victor of the debate, he had to flee Spain because of the resulting persecution. He moved to Israel and helped reestablish communal life in Jerusalem. He authored a classic commentary on the Pentateuch and a commentary on the Talmud.

Nachmanides, Pirush Haramban Bamidbar ad loc.

בעבור שצוה אותם לראות השמנה היא אם רזה, השיבו לו כי היא שמנה וגם זבת חלב ודבש היא, ועל שאלתו היש בה עץ אם אין, השיבו לו "וזה פריה", כי כן צוה אותם להראותו.

והנה בכל זה אמרו אמת והשיבו על מה שנצטוו. והיה להם לאמר שהעם היושב עליה עז והערים בצורות, כי יש להם להשיב אמרי אמת לשולחם, כי כן צוה אותם החזק הוא הרפה הבמחנים אם במבצרים. אבל רשעם במלת "אפס", שהיא מורה על דבר אפס ונמנע מן האדם שאי אפשר בשום ענין.

Moses instructed the spies to check whether or not the land was lush or paltry, and they dutifully reported back that it was lush, flowing with milk and honey. As for Moses' question whether or not it produced fruits, they showed him the fruit of land—exactly as instructed.

With their report, the spies told the truth and simply followed instructions. They were indeed beholden to report back regarding the strength of the inhabitants and status of the fortified cities, for Moses asked these very questions and they were bound to tell the truth to their dispatcher.

Their sin was the additional word, "However [the people who inhabit the land are mighty]." This word connotes a sense of impossibility, [as the spies concluded] that it was impossible for anyone [to conquer the land].

2. Inferiority Complex

Don't Reckon with Public Opinion

TEXT 5

Rabbi Menachem Mendel of Kotzk, Emet M'Kotzk Titzmach p. 177

את הטענה ונהיה בעינינו כחגבים אפשר להבין אולם וכן היינו
בעיניהם טענה זו היא בכלל חטאי המרגלים כי מה מהם יהלוך מה הם
בעיני זולתם.

The claim, "In our eyes, we seemed like grass-hoppers," is understandable. However, the claim of "And so we were in their eyes" is part of the spies' sin—for what difference does it make how someone else views you?!

Positive Attention

TEXT 6

Rabbi Yaakov Yosef of Polonya, Toldos Yaakov Yosef, Parashat Haazinu

"ואיש לא יעלה עמך" רוצה לומר שידמה במחשבתו שהוא לבדו עומד
ומתפלל לפניו יתברך ואין איש עמו שיהיה מתפאר לפניו. והוא הדין
בעסק התורה שילמד רק לפניו יתברך. והוא הדין בגמילות חסדים
שנותן צדקה יכוין רק לפניו יתבך ולא להתפאר.

The verse states, *"And no man shall ascend [Mt. Sinai] with you [Moses]."* This means that when one prays, he should imagine himself alone before G-d, with no other person with him in front of whom to boast. Similarly, when one learns Torah, he should study as if he is alone before G-d. The same applies to being kind to another: When he gives charity, he should imagine himself alone before G-d and not be doing it for self-aggrandizement.

Rabbi Yaakov Yosef of Polnoye

ca. 1710–1784
Chasidic pioneer and author. Rabbi Yaakov Yosef was a dedicated disciple of the Ba'al Shem Tov, the founder of the Chasidic movement, and is credited with taking a leading role in the dissemination of the philosophy of Chasidism in its nascent years. He authored *Toladot Ya'kov Yosef*, the first printed work of Chasidic philosophy. This work is cherished in Chasidic circles.

It's in Your Head

TEXT 7

Rabbi Yehudah Aryeh Leib Alter

(Sefat Emet)

1847–1905

Chasidic master and scholar. Rabbi Yehudah Aryeh Leib Alter assumed the leadership of the Chasidic dynasty of Gur (Gora), a town near Warsaw, Poland, at the age of 23. He was the grandson and successor of Rabbi Yitschak Meir of Gur, the founder of the Gur dynasty. He is commonly referred to as the *Sefat Emet*, after the title of his commentaries on the Torah and Talmud.

Rabbi Yehudah Aryeh Leib Alter of Gur,
Sefat Emet Likutim, Bamidbar ad loc.

נראה הפירוש שלפי שהיינו בעינינו כחגבים, לכן כן היינו בעיניהם, וזהו שאמר המדרש שאם היו מאמינים בה' היו באמת כמאלכים, רק על ידי חסרון אמונה נשפלו גם בעיניהם.

The explanation is as follows: Because they felt that "In our eyes, we seemed like grasshoppers," that is why "and so we were in their eyes." This, then, is the intent of the Midrash which states that if the Jews would have believed in G-d, they would have appeared as angels [to the inhabitants]. It was due to their lack of faith alone that they were seen as lowly in the eyes of the Canaanites.

Jewish Pride

TEXT 8

The Lubavitcher Rebbe, Sichot Kodesh 5726 p. 254

When there is a situation of "In our eyes, we seemed like grasshoppers"; when a person feels the opposite of "Be not afraid of sudden terror or of the darkness of the wicked" and is instead waiting for the wicked one to give him confirmation and applaud him... this is a terrible situation. This undermines the very existence of the Jewish nation.

Such an attitude truly makes no sense! Mordechai is sitting in the king's court, Achashverosh instructed the Temple to be rebuilt, and what did Achashverosh pride himself with? –the holy effects of the Temple! Yet the Jews came, and what were they proud of? –that Achashverosh had invited them to the party!?

Rabbi Menachem Mendel Schneerson
1902–1994
The towering Jewish leader of the 20th century, known as "the Lubavitcher Rebbe," or simply as "the Rebbe." Born in southern Ukraine, the Rebbe escaped Nazi occupied Europe, arriving in the U.S. in June 1941. The Rebbe inspired and guided the revival of traditional Judaism after the European devastation, impacting virtually every Jewish community the world over. The Rebbe often emphasized that the performance of just one additional good deed could usher in the era of Mashiach. The Rebbe's scholarly talks and writings have been printed in more than 200 volumes.

The Rebbe and Israel

TEXT 9

The Lubavitcher Rebbe, Sichot Kodesh 5739 vol. 3 p. 305-6

There is a wonderful message contained within the remarkable story of Zelafchad's daughters... The Torah tells us the background of the story, that Zelafchad's daughters had cherished the land in a unique way, contrary to others of the time who did not demonstrate such affection... They demanded, "Give us a portion in the land!"

The message is that when the Jews demonstrate a proud affection for the land and demand their rights to *it, they are granted their wish. Zelafchad's daughters merited to build homes in Israel...*

The drive to inhabit the land is not limited to those who find themselves outside of Israel... it applies to one who finds himself in the legal borders of the lands as well...

The exile expresses itself chiefly in the fact that the inhabitants of the land listen to foreign influences and are afraid of the nations around them.... They are brainwashed to think that they must find favor in the eyes of the nations and appease them, bowing to international pressure and giving away what belongs to them, wishfully convincing themselves and others that such measures will appease the nations and stabilize the region. This is contrary to the Torah's teachings... This is how it works with the nations of the world: When [Israel] feels, "as grasshoppers in its own eyes," it causes "so we were in their eyes"—and who negotiates with a grasshopper?!

3. Courage from Faith

Trust Brings Strength

TEXT 10

Rashi Bamidbar 14:9

"אַל תִּמְרֹדוּ". וְשׁוּב וְאַתֶּם אַל תִּירָאוּ.

" **Y**ou shall not rebel." And consequently, "You will not fear...."

Rabbi Shlomo Yitschaki (Rashi)
1040–1105
Most noted biblical and Talmudic commentator. Born in Troyes, France, Rashi studied in the famed *yeshivot* of Mainz and Worms. His commentaries on the Pentateuch and the Talmud, which focus on the straightforward meaning of the text, have appeared in virtually every edition of the Talmud and Bible.

TEXT 11

The Lubavitcher Rebbe, Sichot Kodesh 5737 vol. 2 p. 73-75

When a Jew goes out into the world, he indeed does not rely in miracles and takes his "horse and chariot" and military along. Yet, he places his primary trust in G-d...

Even when he engages in the work of the tribe of Zevulun, namely in the world of business, engaging in common civil activity as do all nations of the world, he must go with a triumphant attitude: He goes with the *strength of G-d Who is the master of this world. Yes, this G-d does not want him to rely on miracles and instructs him to work with the sweat of his own palms, but the work is relegated to his hands alone. His head is reserved for loftier pursuits of Torah and* mitzvot, *and his hands are only a tool for G-d's blessing…*

As it is with the individual, so it is with the community… Not only when interacting with coreligionists… but even when interacting with people of other faiths, we must behave with a triumphant approach. Of course, the law of the land is to be respected, but at the same time, we must act as free men…

G-d sees that we are situated in a deep, dark exile where His presence is not felt. So, from time to time, He sends signals that demonstrate how we must conduct ourselves in a triumphant manner, and that it is the only way to overcome all adversaries—both open and covert.

When people see that Jews stand tall and proud—of course in a peaceful manner—this instills respect and brings about a favorable disposition to the Jewish nation. This can only come about when we stand tall as the servants of G-d, the King of all Kings.

TEXT 12

Chief Rabbi Jonathan Sacks, Address to the International Conference of Chabad Shluchim, 2011

Non-Jews respect Jews who respect Judaism.

And non-Jews are embarrassed by Jews who are embarrassed by Judaism.

The Rebbe taught us how to fulfill verau kol amei haaretz ki shem Hashem nikra alecha. *Let all the world see we are never ashamed to stand tall as Jews.*

Rabbi Jonathan Sacks, PhD

1948–

Former chief rabbi of the United Kingdom. Rabbi Sacks attended Cambridge University and received his doctorate from King's College, London. A prolific and influential author, his books include *Will We Have Jewish Grandchildren?* and *The Dignity of Difference.* He received the Jerusalem Prize in 1995 for his contributions to enhancing Jewish life in the Diaspora, was knighted and made a life peer in 2005, and became Baron Sacks of Aldridge in 2009.

In our Personal Lives

TEXT 13

The Lubavitcher Rebbe, Igrot Kodesh vol. 14 p. 156

במה שכותב אודות הקישוים ההעלמות וההסתרים, בודאי שמע על דרך הרמז של הכתוב "ונהי בעינינו כחגבים (על ידי זה ולכן) וכן היינו בעיניהם". ולו הכירו יראי ה' בכלל והחסידים ביחוד את הכחות אשר ניתנו להם, היו נגשים לכל ענין באומץ לב שלא בערך מאשר עתה, ובדרך ממילא היו בטלים כמה העלמות והסתרים וגם קישוים.

You write that you face various challenges and obstacles. Certainly you have heard the homily on the verse, "In our eyes, we seemed like grasshoppers, (and because of that,) and so we were in their eyes." If those who fear G-d, and particularly the Chasidim, would only recognize the tremendous capabilities they are endowed with, they would tackle everything with an entirely different degree of confidence and courage. Organically, the challenges and obstacles would fall away.

TEXT 14

Ibid. vol. 15 p. 263

במענה על מכתבו מכ"ט סיון, כבר ידוע פירוש איזה מהמפרשים על הכתוב, ונהי בעינינו כחגבים, - ורק על ידי זה - וכן היינו בעיניהם, זאת אומרת שכאשר בני ישראל החרדים לדבר ה' ודבקים על ידי תורתו ומצותיו באלקים חיים, מכירים כחם ויכולתם, על ידי זה עצמו מתבטלים כמה העלמות והסתרים, וניתוספת הצלחה בעבודה בהחזקת היהדות האמיתית והפצתה.

In response to your letter from the 29th of Sivan. There is a well-known explanation to the verse, "In our eyes, we seemed like grasshoppers—and because of that—and so we were in their eyes." In other words: When Jews who hearken to G-d's word and cling to His Torah and mitzvot recognize their strength and capabilities, that itself dispels much challenge and adversary, and additional success is achieved in the efforts to strengthen and spread Judaism.

Ants and Grasshoppers

TEXT 15A

Rashi, Bamdibar 13:33

"וכן היינו בעיניהם". שמענו אומרים זה לזה נמלים יש בכרמים כאנשים.

"**A**nd so we were in their eyes." We heard them telling each other, "There are ants in the vineyard who look like people."

TEXT 15B

Mishlei (Proverbs) 6:6-8

לֵךְ אֶל נְמָלָה עָצֵל רְאֵה דְרָכֶיהָ וַחֲכָם:
אֲשֶׁר אֵין לָהּ קָצִין שֹׁטֵר וּמֹשֵׁל:
תָּכִין בַּקַּיִץ לַחְמָהּ אָגְרָה בַקָּצִיר מַאֲכָלָהּ:

Go to the ant, you sluggard; see her ways and become wise.

For she has no chief, overseer, or ruler.

Yet she prepares her bread in the summer; she gathers her food in the harvest.

TEXT 15C

Rabbi Levi Yitzchak of Berditchev, Kedushat Levi, Bamidbar Ibid.

Rabbi Levi Yitschak of Berditchev

1740–1809

Chasidic rebbe. Rabbi Levi Yitschak was one of the foremost disciples of the Magid of Mezeritch and later went on to serve as rabbi in Berditchev, Ukraine. His Chasidic commentary on the Torah, *Kedushat Levi*, is a classic that is popular to this day. He is known in Jewish history and folklore for his all-encompassing love, compassion, and advocacy on behalf of the Jewish people.

"ונהי בעינינו כחגבים וכן היינו בעיניהם". פירש רש"י "שמענו אומרים 'נמלים' יש בכרמים".

ולכאורה קשה הלא בפסוק כתיב "חגבים"?...

וזהו שרמז רש"י בכאן כי המרגלים פרקו מעליהם עול מלכותו יתברך, וזה שפירש רש"י ז"ל "נמלים", כמאמר הפסוק "לך אל נמלה כו' אשר אין לה' כו'", לרמז על הנ"ל.

> **"I**n our eyes, we seemed like grasshoppers." Rashi explains, "We heard them telling each other, 'There are ants in the vineyard who look like people.'"

Why did Rashi deviate from the wording of the verse which reads "grasshoppers?"…

Rashi hints to the fact that the spies' rejected the yoke of heaven. Thus, he uses the word "ants," as in the verse, "Go to the ant…For she has no chief"—to allude to their [rejection of Divine authority].

10

KORACH

The Jewish Spring

How to Stage a Rebellion

Student Manual

PARSHA OVERVIEW
Korach

Korach incites a mutiny challenging Moses' leadership and the granting of the kehunah (priesthood) to Aaron. He is accompanied by Moses' inveterate foes, Dathan and Abiram. Joining them are 250 distinguished members of the community, who offer the sacrosanct ketoret (incense) to prove their worthiness for the priesthood. The earth opens up and swallows the mutineers, and a fire consumes the ketoret-offerers.

A subsequent plague is stopped by Aaron's offering of ketoret. Aaron's staff miraculously blossoms and brings forth almonds, to prove that his designation as high priest is divinely ordained.

G-d commands that a terumah ("uplifting") from each crop of grain, wine and oil, as well as all firstborn sheep and cattle, and other specified gifts, be given to the kohanim *(priests).*

1. Rebellion and Revolt

Korach

TEXT 1

Bamidbar (Numbers) 16:1-4

וַיִּקַּח קֹרַח בֶּן יִצְהָר בֶּן קְהָת בֶּן לֵוִי וְדָתָן וַאֲבִירָם בְּנֵי אֱלִיאָב וְאוֹן בֶּן פֶּלֶת בְּנֵי רְאוּבֵן: וַיָּקֻמוּ לִפְנֵי מֹשֶׁה וַאֲנָשִׁים מִבְּנֵי יִשְׂרָאֵל חֲמִשִּׁים וּמָאתָיִם נְשִׂיאֵי עֵדָה קְרִאֵי מוֹעֵד אַנְשֵׁי שֵׁם: וַיִּקָּהֲלוּ עַל מֹשֶׁה וְעַל אַהֲרֹן וַיֹּאמְרוּ אֲלֵהֶם רַב לָכֶם כִּי כָל הָעֵדָה כֻּלָּם קְדֹשִׁים וּבְתוֹכָם יְקֹוָק וּמַדּוּעַ תִּתְנַשְּׂאוּ עַל קְהַל ה': וַיִּשְׁמַע מֹשֶׁה וַיִּפֹּל עַל פָּנָיו:

Korach the son of Izhar, the son of Kehot, the son of Levi took [himself to one side] along with Dathan and Abiram, the sons of Eliab, and On the son of Peleth, descendants of Reuben.

They confronted Moses together with two hundred and fifty men from the children of Israel, chieftains of the congregation, representatives of the assembly, men of repute.

They assembled against Moses and Aaron, and said to them, "You take too much upon yourselves, for the entire congregation are all holy, and G-d is in their midst. So why do you raise yourselves above G-d's assembly?"

Moses heard and fell on his face.

Timing

TEXT 2A

Rabbi Avraham Ibn Ezra, ad loc.

Rabbi Avraham ibn Ezra
1092–1167

Biblical commentator, linguist and poet. Ibn Ezra was born in Tuledo, Spain and fled the Almohad regime to other parts of Europe. It is believed that he was living in London at the time of his death. Ibn Ezra is best known for his literalistic commentary on the Pentateuch. He also wrote works of poetry, philosophy, medicine, astronomy, and other topics.

זה הדבר היה במדבר סיני כאשר נתחלפו הבכורים ונבדלו הלויים. כי חשבו ישראל שמשה אדוננו עשה מדעתו לתת גדולה לאחיו, גם לבני קהת שהם קרובים אליו ולכל בני לוי שהם ממשפחתו. והלויים קשרו עליו [קרח ומשפחתו] בעבור היותם נתונים לאהרן ובניו... גם קרח בכור היה... ואלה נשיאי העדה היו בכורים.

This matter occurred in the Sinai Desert when the firstborns were replaced by the Priests. The Israelites thought that Moses had made this change of his own accord, in order to raise his brother [Aaron] to greatness, as well as [to give greatness] to the family of Kehot and all of the tribe of Levi who were his relatives. As for the Levites [Korach and his family – who were seemingly the beneficiaries], they rebelled for they were subjugated to Aaron and his sons... also Korach was a firstborn... and these chieftains were firstborns.

TEXT 2B

Rabbi Moshe ben Nachman
(Nachmanides, Ramban)
1194–1270
Scholar, philosopher, author
and physician. Nachmanides
was born in Spain and served
as leader of Iberian Jewry. In
1263, he was summoned by
King James of Aragon to a
public disputation with Pablo
Cristiani, a Jewish apostate.
Though Nachmanides was the
clear victor of the debate, he
had to flee Spain because of
the resulting persecution. He
moved to Israel and helped
reestablish communal life
in Jerusalem. He authored
a classic commentary
on the Pentateuch and a
commentary on the Talmud.

Nachmanides, Pirush Haramban, ad loc.

זה מדעתו של רבי אברהם, שהוא אומר במקומות רבים אין מוקדם
ומאוחר בתורה. וכבר כתבתי כי על דעתי כל התורה כסדר, זולתי במקום
אשר יפרש הכתוב ההקדמה והאיחור.

אבל היה הדבר הזה במדבר פארן בקדש ברנע אחרי חטא המרגלים...
שכעס קרח על נשיאות אלצפן וקינא גם באהרן כמו שנאמר ובקשתם
גם כהונה.

והנה ישראל במדבר סיני לא אירע להם שום רעה, כי גם בדבר העגל
שהיה החטא גדול ומפורסם היו המתים מועטים וניצלו בתפילתו של
משה שהתנפל עליהם ארבעים יום וארבעים לילה. והנה היו אוהבים
אותו כנפשם ושומעים אליו ואילו היה אדם מורד על משה בזמן ההוא,
היו העם סוקלים אותו. ולכן סבל קורח גדולת אהרן וסבלו הבכורים
מעלת הלויים וכל מעשיו של משה.

וכאשר חטאו במרגלים לא התפלל משה עליהם... ונגזר על כל העם
שיתמו במדבר ושם ימותו, אז היתה נפש כל העם מרה והיו אומרים
בליבם כי יבואו להם מדברי משה תקלות! ואז מצא קורח מקום לחלוק
על מעשי משה וחשב כי ישמעו אליו העם.

T his is the opinion of the Ibn Ezra, who often states that there is not necessarily any chronological order to the Torah. However, as I have written in the past, the Torah is actually in chronological sequence (except where the verse clearly departs from it).

Rather, this matter took place in Midbar Paran, in Kadesh Barnea, after the sin of the Spies... Korach was angry about the appointment of Eltzafon to the *leadership of the Kehot family, and was also jealous about Aaron, as it states, "And now you seek the kehunah as well?"*

No bad befell the Jews while they were in the desert. Even the Golden Calf episode, which was the great and notorious sin, did not involve many fatalities; the people were saved by Moses, who prayed for them for forty days and nights. They loved Moses as much as they loved themselves, and listened to him; if anyone had defied Moses in that period, the people would have stoned him. So Korach was forced to tolerate Aaron's preeminence, and the firstborns were forced to tolerate the promotion of the Levites, and all of Moses' actions.

However, when the people sinned in the episode of the Spies, Moses did not pray for them... it was decreed that the entire people would perish in the desert. It was then that the people first rebelled and said to themselves that Moses' words result in misfortune. Korach seized the opportunity to fight against Moses and hope that the people would side with him.

Dathan and Abiram

TEXT 3A

Devarim (Deuteronomy) 11:6

וַאֲשֶׁר עָשָׂה לְדָתָן וְלַאֲבִירָם בְּנֵי אֱלִיאָב בֶּן רְאוּבֵן אֲשֶׁר פָּצְתָה הָאָרֶץ אֶת פִּיהָ וַתִּבְלָעֵם וְאֶת בָּתֵּיהֶם וְאֶת אָהֳלֵיהֶם וְאֵת כָּל הַיְקוּם אֲשֶׁר בְּרַגְלֵיהֶם בְּקֶרֶב כָּל יִשְׂרָאֵל:

And what He did to Dathan and Abiram, sons of Eliab, the son of Reuben, that the earth opened its mouth and swallowed them up and their households and their tents, and all the possessions at their feet, in the midst of all Israel.

TEXT 3B

Tehillim (Psalms) 106:16-17

וַיְקַנְאוּ לְמֹשֶׁה בַּמַּחֲנֶה לְאַהֲרֹן קְדוֹשׁ ה':
תִּפְתַּח אֶרֶץ וַתִּבְלַע דָּתָן וַתְּכַס עַל עֲדַת אֲבִירָם:

They angered Moses in the camp, Aaron, the holy man of G-d.

The earth opened up and swallowed Dathan and covered the congregation of Abiram.

TEXT 4

Ibn Ezra Ibid.

וקשר דתן ואבירם בעבור ש[יעקב אבינו] הסיר הבכורה מראובן אביהם
ונתנה ליוסף, אולי חשדוהו בעבור יהושע משרתו [שהיה משבט יוסף].

Dathan and Abiram's connection was that Jacob had removed the firstborn status from Reuben their ancestor and given it to Joseph. Perhaps, here too, they suspected Moses of doing the same, as he favored Joshua (from the tribe of Joseph) as his assistant.

Age-Old Anarchists

TEXT 5A

Shemot (Exudos) 2:11-15

וַיְהִי בַּיָּמִים הָהֵם וַיִּגְדַּל מֹשֶׁה וַיֵּצֵא אֶל אֶחָיו וַיַּרְא בְּסִבְלֹתָם וַיַּרְא אִישׁ
מִצְרִי מַכֶּה אִישׁ עִבְרִי מֵאֶחָיו:
וַיִּפֶן כֹּה וָכֹה וַיַּרְא כִּי אֵין אִישׁ וַיַּךְ אֶת הַמִּצְרִי וַיִּטְמְנֵהוּ בַּחוֹל:
וַיֵּצֵא בַּיּוֹם הַשֵּׁנִי וְהִנֵּה שְׁנֵי אֲנָשִׁים עִבְרִים נִצִּים וַיֹּאמֶר לָרָשָׁע לָמָּה
תַכֶּה רֵעֶךָ:
וַיֹּאמֶר מִי שָׂמְךָ לְאִישׁ שַׂר וְשֹׁפֵט עָלֵינוּ הַלְהָרְגֵנִי אַתָּה אֹמֵר כַּאֲשֶׁר הָרַגְתָּ
אֶת הַמִּצְרִי וַיִּירָא מֹשֶׁה וַיֹּאמַר אָכֵן נוֹדַע הַדָּבָר:
וַיִּשְׁמַע פַּרְעֹה אֶת הַדָּבָר הַזֶּה וַיְבַקֵּשׁ לַהֲרֹג אֶת מֹשֶׁה וַיִּבְרַח מֹשֶׁה מִפְּנֵי
פַרְעֹה וַיֵּשֶׁב בְּאֶרֶץ מִדְיָן וַיֵּשֶׁב עַל הַבְּאֵר:

Now it came to pass in those days that Moses grew up and went out to his brothers and looked at their burdens, and he saw an Egyptian man striking a Hebrew man of his brothers.

He turned this way and that way, and he saw that there was no man; so he struck the Egyptian and hid him in the sand.

He went out on the second day, and behold, two Hebrew men were quarreling, and he said to the wicked one, "Why are you going to strike your friend?"

And he retorted, "Who made you a man, a prince, and a judge over us? Do you plan to slay me as you have slain the Egyptian?" Moses became frightened and said, "Indeed, the matter has become known!"

Pharaoh heard of this incident, and he sought to slay Moses; so Moses fled from before Pharaoh. He stayed in the land of Midian, and he sat down by a well.

TEXT 5B

Rashi ad loc.

Rabbi Shlomo Yitschaki
(Rashi)
1040–1105
Most noted biblical and
Talmudic commentator.
Born in Troyes, France,
Rashi studied in the famed
yeshivot of Mainz and
Worms. His commentaries
on the Pentateuch and the
Talmud, which focus on the
straightforward meaning
of the text, have appeared
in virtually every edition
of the Talmud and Bible.

"שני אנשים עברים". דתן ואבירם הם שהותירו מן המן.
"וישמע פרעה". הם הלשינו עליו.

"**T**wo Hebrew men were quarreling."
Dathan and Abiram. They were the
ones who saved some of the manna
[although G-d forbade it].

"Pharaoh heard." They informed on him.

TEXT 6

Midrash Shemot Rabah 1:29

Shemot Rabah
An early rabbinic commentary
on the Book of Exodus. The
term "Midrash" is derived
from the root d-r-sh, which
means "to search," "to
examine," and "to investigate."
Shemot Rabah, written
mostly in Hebrew, provides
textual exegeses, expounds
upon the biblical narrative,
and develops and illustrates
moral principles. It was first
published in Constantinople in
1512 together with four other
Midrashic works on the other
four books of the Pentateuch.

אתה מוצא שלא נשמע הדבר אלא על ידי עברים, שנאמר ויצא ביום
השני והנה שני אנשים עברים—זה דתן ואבירם... הם הם שאמרו דבר זה,
הם היו שהותירו מן המן, הם היו שאמרו 'נתנה ראש ונשובה מצרימה'".

It emerges that the matter [of Moses' killing the
Egyptian] only became known because of Jews,
as it says, "And he went out on the second day and
two Jewish men"—these are Dathan and Abiram… It
was they who told over this information, it was they
who left over manna, and it was they who said [after
the report of the spies], "Let us appoint a leader and let
us return to Egypt."

Spiritual Counterbalance

TEXT 7

Rabbi Yehudah Loew
(Maharal of Prague)
1525–1609

Talmudist and philosopher.
Maharal rose to prominence
as leader of the famed Jewish
community of Prague. He
is the author of more than
a dozen works of original
philosophic thought, including
Tiferet Yisrael and *Netsach
Yisrael*. He also authored *Gur
Aryeh*, a supercommentary to
Rashi's biblical commentary,
and a commentary on the non-
legal passages of the Talmud.
He is buried in the Old
Jewish Cemetery of Prague.

Rabbi Yehudah Loew of Prague, Gevurot Hashem ch. 19

דתן ואבירם לעולם רצועת מרדות למשה ולישראל... כי כאשר זכו
ישראל לשני אנשים נבדלים מכלל ישראל במעלה והם משה ואהרן,
[הנה] זה לעומת זה היה מישראל ב' אנשים רשעים נבדלים לרע,
מתנגדים תמיד למשה ולתורתו.

Dathan and Abiram were a constant source of trouble for Moses and the Jewish people… Because the Jewish people merited to have two great men, unique from the rest of the people, namely Moses and Aaron, there was to be the counterbalance—two wicked men, unique in their evil, constantly opposing against Moses and his teaching.

2. Care and Concern

Moshe's Response

TEXT 8A

Bamidbar (Numbers) 16:8-10

וַיֹּאמֶר מֹשֶׁה אֶל קֹרַח שִׁמְעוּ נָא בְּנֵי לֵוִי:
הַמְעַט מִכֶּם כִּי הִבְדִּיל אֱלֹהֵי יִשְׂרָאֵל אֶתְכֶם מֵעֲדַת יִשְׂרָאֵל לְהַקְרִיב
אֶתְכֶם אֵלָיו לַעֲבֹד אֶת עֲבֹדַת מִשְׁכַּן ה' וְלַעֲמֹד לִפְנֵי הָעֵדָה לְשָׁרְתָם:
וַיַּקְרֵב אֹתְךָ וְאֶת כָּל אַחֶיךָ בְנֵי לֵוִי אִתָּךְ וּבִקַּשְׁתֶּם גַּם כְּהֻנָּה:

Moses said to Korach, "Please listen, sons of Levi.

"Is it not enough that the G-d of Israel has distinguished you from the congregation of Israel to draw you near to Him, to perform the service in the Mishkan of G-d and to stand before the congregation to minister to them?

"He drew you near, and all your brothers, the sons of Levi with you, and now you seek the kehunah as well?"

TEXT 8B

Ibid. 16:12-14

וַיִּשְׁלַח מֹשֶׁה לִקְרֹא לְדָתָן וְלַאֲבִירָם בְּנֵי אֱלִיאָב וַיֹּאמְרוּ לֹא נַעֲלֶה:

הַמְעַט כִּי הֶעֱלִיתָנוּ מֵאֶרֶץ זָבַת חָלָב וּדְבַשׁ לַהֲמִיתֵנוּ בַּמִּדְבָּר כִּי תִשְׂתָּרֵר עָלֵינוּ גַּם הִשְׂתָּרֵר:

אַף לֹא אֶל אֶרֶץ זָבַת חָלָב וּדְבַשׁ הֲבִיאֹתָנוּ וַתִּתֶּן לָנוּ נַחֲלַת שָׂדֶה וָכָרֶם הַעֵינֵי הָאֲנָשִׁים הָהֵם תְּנַקֵּר לֹא נַעֲלֶה:

Moses sent to call Dathan and Abiram, the sons of Eliab, but they said, "We will not go up.

"Is it not enough that you have brought us out of a land flowing with milk and honey to kill us in the desert, that you should also exercise authority over us?

"You have not even brought us to a land flowing with milk and honey, nor have you given us an inheritance of fields and vineyards. Even if you gouge out the eyes of those men, we will not go up."

TEXT 8C

Ibid. 16:15

וַיִּחַר לְמֹשֶׁה מְאֹד וַיֹּאמֶר אֶל ה' אַל תֵּפֶן אֶל מִנְחָתָם לֹא חֲמוֹר אֶחָד מֵהֶם נָשָׂאתִי וְלֹא הֲרֵעֹתִי אֶת אַחַד מֵהֶם:

Moses was exceedingly distressed, and he said to G-d, "Do not accept their offering. I have not taken a donkey from a single one of them, and I have not harmed a single one of them."

TEXT 9A

Ibid 16:24

דַּבֵּר אֶל הָעֵדָה לֵאמֹר הֵעָלוּ מִסָּבִיב לְמִשְׁכַּן קֹרַח דָּתָן וַאֲבִירָם:

"Speak to the congregation saying, 'Withdraw from the dwelling of Korach, Dathan, and Abiram.'"

TEXT 9B

Ibid. 16:25

וַיָּקָם מֹשֶׁה וַיֵּלֶךְ אֶל דָּתָן וַאֲבִירָם וַיֵּלְכוּ אַחֲרָיו זִקְנֵי יִשְׂרָאֵל:

Moses arose and went to Dathan and Abiram, and the elders of Israel followed him.

TEXT 9C

Bamidar Rabah

An exegetical commentary on the first seven chapters of the book of Numbers and a homiletic commentary on the rest of the book. The first part of *Bamidbar Rabah* is notable for its inclusion of esoteric material; the second half is essentially identical to *Midrash Tanchuma* on the book of Numbers. It was first published in Constantinople in 1512, together with four other midrashic works on the other four books of the Pentateuch.

Midrash Bamidbar Rabah 18:12

אף על פי ששמע משה מפי הגבורה, לא אמר להם 'העלו' עד שהלך והתרה בהם.

Even though Moses had heard from G-d [to clear the area], he was not going to make the order to evacuate until he went and warned them.

TEXT 9D

Rabbi Shmuel Eliezer Halevi Eidel's, Maharsha Sanhedrin 110a

Rabbi Shmuel Eliezer Halevi Eidel's

(Maharsha)
1555–1632

Rabbi, author, and Talmudist. Rabbi Eidel's established a yeshivah in Posen, Poland, which was supported by his mother-in-law, Eidel (hence his surname is "Eidel's"). He is primarily known for his *Chidushei Halachot,* a commentary on the Talmud in which he resolves difficulties in the texts of the Talmud, Rashi, and *Tosafot,* and which is a basic work for those who seek an in-depth understanding of the Talmud; and for his *Chidushei Agadot,* his innovative commentary on the homiletic passages of the Talmud.

הלך משה בעצמו לדבר עמם דברי ריצוי אולי ישובו.

Moses himself went to speak to them appeasing words, in the hope that they would repent.

TEXT 10

Rashi, Bamidbar ad loc.

"ויקם משה". כסבור שישאו לו פנים.

"Moses arose." He thought they would show him respect, but they did not.

TEXT 11

The Lubavitcher Rebbe, Likutei Sichot vol. 28 p. 101-102

Rabbi Menachem Mendel Schneerson
1902–1994
The towering Jewish leader of the 20th century, known as "the Lubavitcher Rebbe," or simply as "the Rebbe." Born in southern Ukraine, the Rebbe escaped Nazi occupied Europe, arriving in the U.S. in June 1941. The Rebbe inspired and guided the revival of traditional Judaism after the European devastation, impacting virtually every Jewish community the world over. The Rebbe often emphasized that the performance of just one additional good deed could usher in the era of Mashiach. The Rebbe's scholarly talks and writings have been printed in more than 200 volumes.

רש"י האט שוין פריער מפרש געווען, אופן פסוק "ויקם שדה עפרון"—"תקומה היתה לו". דאס הייסט, אז "ויקם" ווייזט (אויך) אויף קימה ועליה. ועל דרך זה בעניננו... משה איז ניט סתם געגאנגען צו משכן דתן ואבירם, נאר דאס איז געווען אינעם אופן פון "ויקם משה (וילך)"—"תקומה היתה לו", אז ס'איז געווען ווי די הליכה פון א מלך ומרומם מעם, וואס רופט ארויס א רגש של חשיבות וכבוד—און זיין כוונה דערביי איז געווען—"כסבור שישאו לו פנים", אז דאס וועט פועל זיין ביי דתן ואבירם "שישאו לו פנים"...

לויט דעם ביאור איז אויך אויף פארענטפערט די קושיא הנ"ל—ווי אזוי האט משה זיך אפגעהאלטן פון צו מקיים זיין באלד דעם ציווי ה' און האט זיך פארנומען מיט אן אנדער ענין?

וההסברה: לויט רש"י איז די הליכת משה ניט געווען אויף צו מתרה זיין דתן ואבירם; ואדרבה: לויט פשוטו של מקרא דארף אויסקומען, אז משה האט גאר ניט געטארט גיין מתרה זיין דתן ואבירם און משתדל זיין זיי מחזיר זיין בתשובה—ווייל דאס איז היפך ציווי ה'...

נאר דער מכוון ותכלית פון דער הליכה ("וילך אל דתן ואבירם") איז געווען צו ווארענען די עדה, אז זיי זאלן זיך אפקערן "מעל אהלי האנשים וגו'";

ס'איז נאר וואס די הליכה איז געווען אינעם אופן פון "ויקם משה", בכדי "שישאו לו פנים"—טראכטנדיק אז אפשר וועט אזא הליכה גורם זיין אז "ישאו לו פנים".

Rashi previously commented on the verse, *"The field of Efron arose" that "It experienced an elevation." Meaning, the word "arose" indicates a rise of stature. So it is in our case... Moses did not simply go from the* Mishkan *to Dathan and Abiram;*

rather, he did it in a manner of arising, of experiencing an elevation. His walk [to Dathan and Abiram] was that of an exalted king who creates an aura of importance and respect. He did this thinking that they would show him respect...

We can now understand how Moshe seemingly delayed carrying out G-d's instructions immediately and did his own thing instead. According to Rashi, Moses did not go to warn them. Indeed, from the verses themselves it is evident that he wasn't allowed to warn them, for that would have been against G-d's instruction...

Moses' walk was in fact to warn the people and instruct them to move away from the tents of these evildoers, as G-d had commanded. Along the way, Moses figured he would go in a very royal manner, hoping that would impress Dathan and Abiram to show him respect.

3. I am Here for You

Moshe's Leadership

TEXT 12A

Shemot (Exodus) 19:14

וַיֵּרֶד מֹשֶׁה מִן הָהָר אֶל הָעָם וַיְקַדֵּשׁ אֶת הָעָם וַיְכַבְּסוּ שִׂמְלֹתָם:

Moses descended from the mountain to the people and he prepared the people, and they washed their garments.

TEXT 12B

Rashi, ad loc.

"מן ההר אל העם". מלמד שלא היה משה פונה לעסקיו אלא מן ההר אל העם.

"From the mountain to the people." [This] teaches [us] that Moses did not turn to his [own] affairs, rather [he went directly] from the mountain to the people.

TEXT 13

The Lubavitcher Rebbe, Likutei Sichot vol. 16 p. 427

דער תפקיד פון א נשיא איז, אז צום אלעם ערשטן דארף ער זיך
משתדל זיין אז אידן זאלן טאן דאס וואס זיי דארפן טאן, און ערשט
דערנאך טראכטן וועגן זיך און זיינע ענינים.

און ווי רש"י האט שוין פריער מפרש געווען אויפן פסוק "וירד משה מן
ההר אל העם"—"מלמד שלא היה משה פונה לעסקיו אלא מן ההר אל
העם"... נאר דער ענין וחידוש איז, "לא היה פונה לעסקיו" [מיינט ניט
(נאר) צו זיינע צרכי הגוף וכו', נאר אויך] צו זיינע עסקים אין דעם ענין
ושליחות גופא—זיינע הכנות צו מתן תורה, כולל אויך (ובפרט) צו זיין
ראוי צו "משה קבל תורה מסיני".

The mandate of a leader is, first and foremost, to ensure that the Jews do what they need to do, and only then to worry about his own needs. As Rashi comments on the words, "Moses descended from the mountain to the people—[This] teaches [us] that Moses did not turn to his [own] affairs"…

Not only did Moses not turn to his own personal needs, but he did not turn to even those matters which pertained to his mission—his own preparation for receiving the Torah in order to be fit for the role of being, "Moses received the Torah from Sinai."

TEXT 14

Midrash Devarim Rabah 2:9

Devarim Rabah

A homiletic commentary on the Book of Deuteronomy. It was first published in Constantinople in 1512, with four other Midrashic works on the other four books of the Pentateuch. The homilies are structured similarly; each episode begins with a question of religious law and is followed by an answer, which opens with the words, "Our sages taught." Most commentaries end with reassurances and promises of the redemption.

אמר הקדוש ברוך הוא למשה: אם אתה נקבר כאן אצלן, בזכותן הן באין עמך.

אמר רבי לוי: למה הדבר דומה? לאחד שנתפזרו מעותיו במקום אפילה. אמר, אם אני אומר האירו לי שאקבץ מעותי, אין בריה משגחת עלי. מה עשה? נטל זהוב אחד והשליך בתוכם והתחיל צווח ואומר: האירו לי, זהוב אחד היה לי ונפל ממני כאן. והאירו לו. מה עשה? משנטל את הזהוב אמר להן: בחייכם המתינו לי שאלקט את המעות וליקטן. בזכות הזהוב, נתלקטו המעות. כך אמר לו הקדוש ברוך הוא למשה: אם נקבר אתה אצלם במדבר, הן באים בזכותך ואתה בא בראשם.

G-d said to Moses: If you will be buried here, they will go [into the Land] in your merit.

Rabbi Levi said: An analogy for this is a man whose coins were scattered about in the dark. He thought to himself, "If I ask people to bring lights so that I can gather my coins, no one will pay attention." So what did he do? He took a piece of gold and threw it into the darkness, and then began to shout, "Bring lights for me! I have lost a piece of gold!" They lit up the place for him, and then when he reclaimed the gold, he said to them, "Surely you will wait while I gather my coins as well." And he gathered them.

Thus, in the merit of the gold piece, the coins were gathered. This is what G-d told Moses: If you will be buried near them, here in the desert, they will enter the Land in your merit, and you will be at their head.

TEXT 15

Babylonian Talmud
A literary work of monumental proportions that draws upon the legal, spiritual, intellectual, ethical, and historical traditions of Judaism. The 37 tractates of the Babylonian Talmud contain the teachings of the Jewish sages from the period after the destruction of the 2nd Temple through the 5th century CE. It has served as the primary vehicle for the transmission of the Oral Law and the education of Jews over the centuries; it is the entry point for all subsequent legal, ethical, and theological Jewish scholarship.

Talmud Tractate Berachot 4a

שמרה נפשי כי חסיד אני... כך אמר דוד לפני הקדוש ברוך הוא: רבונו של עולם, לא חסיד אני?! שכל מלכי מזרח ומערב יושבים אגודות אגודות בכבודם, ואני ידי מלוכלכות בדם ובשפיר ובשליא כדי לטהר אשה לבעלה.

"Watch my soul, for I am pious..." David said to G-d: Master of the world, am I not pious? All the kings of the East and the West sit with much glory among their company, whereas my hands are soiled with blood in an effort to allow a woman to stay with her husband!"

The Rebbe

TEXT 16

Rabbi Yosef Yitzchak of Lubavitch, Igrot Kodesh vol. 15 p. 211

וועד הרבנים בצרפת מתעניין מאוד בשאלת הרבנות ורוצה לדעת אם אפשר לדבר על המועמדות שלך, חתני יקירי... ילדים אהובים! אין לי מילים לבטא איזו שמחה גרמה לי ההצעה הזו וכמה הייתי מאושר לו הייתם מקבלים אותה... הנני פונה אליכם ילדים אהובים לשקול היטב ובעומק את ההצעה".

The rabbinical council in France are intensively looking into finding a rabbi, and want to know if they can speak to you about being a candidate.

My dear son-in-law... my beloved children! I have no words that can express how much joy this offer brings me, and how happy I would be if you accepted it... I ask you, beloved children, to properly consider the offer.

TEXT 17

The Lubavitcher Rebbe, letter dated 26 Adar 5710 (1950)

הגיעני מכתבו מי"ג אדר ונבהלתי בקוראי אותו–לדרוש ממני ענינים
שלא ניתנו לי, ואינם בי, לא מהם ולא ממינם! ואין טענתי על כבוד
תורתו בכך שאינו מכירני פנים אל פנים, אבל חקירה ודרישה היה עליו
לעשות מקודם.

Your letter of 13 Adar reached me and I was shocked as I read it—for it asked of me things that were never granted to me, that are not me, not in any way. I have no complaints that you do not know me personally, but you should have done research beforehand.

Rabbi Yosef Yitschak Schneersohn
(Rayats, Frierdiker Rebbe, Previous Rebbe)
1880–1950

Chasidic rebbe, prolific writer, and Jewish activist. Rabbi Yosef Yitschak, the 6th leader of the Chabad movement, actively promoted Jewish religious practice in Soviet Russia and was arrested for these activities. After his release from prison and exile, he settled in Warsaw, Poland, from where he fled Nazi occupation, and arrived in New York in 1940. Settling in Brooklyn, Rabbi Schneersohn worked to revitalize American Jewish life. His son-in law, Rabbi Menachem Mendel Schneerson, succeeded him as the leader of the Chabad movement.

Conclusion—We are all Leaders

TEXT 18

The Lubavitcher Rebbe, Likutei Sichot vol. 16 p. 432

אצל כל אדם יש את ענין ה'נשיאות' – מה שכל אחד הוא נשיא
בסביבתו, וכאן מגיעה ההוראה שכדי שעבודת ה' שלו תהיה כדבעי,
עליה להיות מעורבת בביטול [ובהתמסרות].

Every person has an element of leadership—the ability of each person to be a leader in his own milieu. And this teaches us a lesson for our own spiritual lives: in order to have proper service of G-d, one's leadership must incorporate self-sacrifice.

11

CHUKAT

Jewish Sparks

What Happened When Moses Hit the Rock

Student Manual

PARSHA OVERVIEW
Chukat

Moses is taught the laws of the red heifer, whose ashes purify a person who has been contaminated by contact with a dead body.

After forty years of journeying through the desert, the people of Israel arrive in the wilderness of Zin. Miriam dies, and the people thirst for water. G-d tells Moses to speak to a rock and command it to give water. Moses gets angry at the rebellious Israelites and strikes the stone. Water issues forth, but Moses is told by G-d that neither he nor Aaron will enter the Promised Land.

Aaron dies at Hor Hahar and is succeeded in the high priesthood by his son Elazar. Venomous snakes attack the Israelite camp after yet another eruption of discontent in which the people "speak against G-d and Moses"; G-d tells Moses to place a brass serpent upon a high pole, and all who will gaze heavenward will be healed. The people sing a song in honor of the miraculous well that provided them water in the desert.

Moses leads the people in battles against the Emorite kings Sichon and Og (who seek to prevent Israel's passage through their territory) and conquers their lands, which lie east of the Jordan.

1. Moshe's Sin

A Story with a Rock

TEXT 1

Rabbi Yitzchak Arama
1420–1494

Spanish rabbi and philosopher; known as "the Ba'al Akeidah," after his work, *Akeidat Yitzchak*, an influential philosophic and mystical commentary on the Torah. After initially serving as head of the yeshivah in Zamora, Spain, he was appointed as rabbi and preacher for the community of Tarragona. His writings were received favorably by his peers, including Rabbi Don Yitzchak Abravanel. After the expulsion of 1492, Rabbi Arama ultimately settled in Naples, where he is buried.

Rabbi Yitzchak Arama, Akeidat Yitzchak, Parashat Chukat ch. 80

הרי שולחן והרי בשר והרי סכין לפנינו – ואין לנו פה לאכול! כי מצות ה' למשה כתובה לפנינו, והמעשה אשר עשה לא נעלם מנגד עינינו – ומחרון אף ה' ישתומם לבנו. ואין איתנו פירוש על זה שישכך את האוזן ביישוב הכתובים.

The table, the meat, and the knife are all here before us—but we have no mouth with which to eat! G-d's commandment to Moses is written before us, the act that was done is not lost before our eyes—yet from G-d's wrath, our hearts are shocked. We know of no interpretation that could soften the blow of reading these verses.

The Holy Troika

TEXT 2

Midrash Shemot Rabah 26:1

"לא שלותי ולא שקטתי ולא נחתי ויבא רוגז"... "לא שלותי" מגזירה
הראשונה שגזר פרעה עלי שנאמר "וימררו את חייהם", והעמיד לו
הקדוש ברוך הוא גואל—זו מרים על שם המירור.

"ולא שקטתי" מגזירה שנייה "אם בן הוא והמתן אותו", והעמיד הקדוש
ברוך הוא גואל—זה אהרן על שם ההריון.

"ולא נחתי" מגזירה שלישית שגזר ואמר "כל הבן הילוד היאורה
תשליכוהו", והעמיד הקדוש ברוך הוא גואל על שם המים—זה משה
שנאמר "כי מן המים משיתיהו".

T he verse states, "I was not at ease, neither was I quiet, and I did not rest, yet trouble came." "I was not at ease" from the first decree that Pharaoh decreed on me, as is says, "And they embittered their lives," and G-d appointed a redeemer—[named] Miriam, on account of "miror (bitterness)."

"I was not quiet" from the second decree of, "If it is a son, you shall put him to death," and G-d appointed a redeemer—[named] Aaron, on account of "hirayon (pregnancy)."

"I did not rest" from the third decree of, "Every son who is born you shall cast into the Nile," and G-d appointed a redeemer—[named] Moses, as it is written "From the water I drew him (mishisuhu)."

Shemot Rabah
An early rabbinic commentary on the Book of Exodus. The term "Midrash" is derived from the root d-r-sh, which means "to search," "to examine," and "to investigate." Shemot Rabah, written mostly in Hebrew, provides textual exegeses, expounds upon the biblical narrative, and develops and illustrates moral principles. It was first published in Constantinople in 1512 together with four other Midrashic works on the other four books of the Pentateuch.

TEXT 3

Babylonian Talmud

A literary work of monumental proportions that draws upon the legal, spiritual, intellectual, ethical, and historical traditions of Judaism. The 37 tractates of the Babylonian Talmud contain the teachings of the Jewish sages from the period after the destruction of the 2nd Temple through the 5th century CE. It has served as the primary vehicle for the transmission of the Oral Law and the education of Jews over the centuries; it is the entry point for all subsequent legal, ethical, and theological Jewish scholarship.

Talmud Tractate Ta'anit 9a

רבי יוסי ברבי יהודה אומר: שלשה פרנסים טובים עמדו לישראל ואלו הן: משה ואהרן ומרים. וג' מתנות טובות ניתנו על ידם ואלו הן: באר וענן ומן, באר בזכות מרים, עמוד ענן בזכות אהרן, מן בזכות משה.

Rabbi Yosi, the son of Rabbi Yehuda, said: Three good patrons rose up for Israel. They were Moses, Aaron, and Miriam. Three good gifts were given on their account and they are: the well, the cloud, and the manna. The well was in the merit of Miriam, the pillar of cloud in the merit of Aaron, and the manna in the merit of Moses.

The Well of Miriam

TEXT 4

Yalkut Shimoni

A Midrash that covers the entire Biblical text. Its material is collected from all over rabbinic literature, including the Babylonian and Jerusalem Talmuds and various ancient Midrashic texts. It contains several passages from Midrashim that have been lost, as well as different versions of existing Midrashim. It is unclear when and by whom this Midrash was redacted.

Midrash Yalkut Shimoni, Bamidbar §683

והבאר בזכות מרים ... והיאך היתה עשויה? כמין סלע והיתה מתגלגלת ובאה עמהם במסעות, וכיון שהיו הדגלים חונים והמשכן עומד, היה בא הסלע ויושב לו בחצר אהל מועד, והנשיאים עומדים על גבו ואומרים: עלי באר, והיתה עולה.

The well was in the merit of Miriam… How was it done? It was a stone which would roll along with them in their travels; when the divisions would stop to camp and the Tabernacle was erected, the stone would come to a rest in the courtyard of the Tent of Meeting. The princes of the tribes would stand on it and say: Well, arise! And it would rise.

TEXT 5

Rabbi Shabetai Bass, Siftei Chachamim Bamidbar ch. 20 §80

ואם תאמר למה לא היה הבאר בזכות אהרן או משה? ויש לומר בזכות שהמתינה למשה על המים לראות מה יעשה לו כשהושלך בתיבה, לכך נעשה לה זכות זה של באר, דהיינו מים שנתן הקדוש ברוך הוא לעדה בשבילה.

W hy was the well not in the merit of Aaron or Moses?

Miriam waited at the riverbank to see what would happen to Moses when he was placed [into the Nile] in a box [as an infant]. That is why the well was created in her merit, that is, the water that G-d provided for the people because of her.

Rabbi Shabetai Bass
1641–1718
Born in Kalisz, Poland, Rabbi Bass was a publisher, bibliographer, and commentator. Rabbi Bass traveled extensively throughout the centers of Jewish scholarship and settled in eastern Germany to establish a printing press for Jewish books. After a number of controversies, he was forced to close down his press. He authored an extensive work of Jewish bibliography, as well as the widely received *Siftei Chachamim* on Rashi.

The Waters of Strife

TEXT 6A

Bamidbar 20:1-4

וַיָּבֹאוּ בְנֵי יִשְׂרָאֵל כָּל הָעֵדָה מִדְבַּר צִן בַּחֹדֶשׁ הָרִאשׁוֹן וַיֵּשֶׁב הָעָם בְּקָדֵשׁ
וַתָּמָת שָׁם מִרְיָם וַתִּקָּבֵר שָׁם:
וְלֹא הָיָה מַיִם לָעֵדָה וַיִּקָּהֲלוּ עַל מֹשֶׁה וְעַל אַהֲרֹן:
וַיָּרֶב הָעָם עִם מֹשֶׁה וַיֹּאמְרוּ לֵאמֹר וְלוּ גָוַעְנוּ בִּגְוַע אַחֵינוּ לִפְנֵי ה':
וְלָמָה הֲבֵאתֶם אֶת קְהַל ה' אֶל הַמִּדְבָּר הַזֶּה לָמוּת שָׁם אֲנַחְנוּ וּבְעִירֵנוּ:

T he entire congregation of the children of Israel arrived at the desert of Zin in the first month, and the people settled in Kadesh. Miriam died there and was buried there.

The congregation had no water; so they assembled against Moses and Aaron.

The people quarreled with Moses, and they said, "If only we had died with the death of our brothers before G-d.

"Why have you brought the congregation of G-d to this desert so that we and our livestock should die there?"

TEXT 6B

Rashi Tractate Ta'anit 9a

שלא היה רוצה להזיל מימיו בשבילו, לפי שמתה מרים.

The well did not want to drip water, for Miriam had died.

Rabbi Shlomo Yitschaki
(Rashi)
1040–1105
Most noted biblical and
Talmudic commentator.
Born in Troyes, France,
Rashi studied in the famed
yeshivot of Mainz and
Worms. His commentaries
on the Pentateuch and the
Talmud, which focus on the
straightforward meaning
of the text, have appeared
in virtually every edition
of the Talmud and Bible.

TEXT 7

Rashi Bamidbar 20:10

"המן הסלע הזה נוציא". לפי שלא היו מכירים אותו, לפי שהלך הסלע
וישב לו בין הסלעים כשנסתלק הבאר.

"Can we draw [water] from this rock?" For the rock had gone and settled among the other rocks when the well departed.

TEXT 8

Bamidar Rabah

An exegetical commentary on the first seven chapters of the book of Numbers and a homiletic commentary on the rest of the book. The first part of *Bamidbar Rabah* is notable for its inclusion of esoteric material; the second half is essentially identical to *Midrash Tanchuma* on the book of Numbers. It was first published in Constantinople in 1512, together with four other midrashic works on the other four books of the Pentateuch.

Midrash Bamidbar Rabah 19:9

התחילו לומר: יודע משה חק הסלע, אם הוא מבקש יוציא לנו מים מזה. נמצא משה עומד בספק אם אשמע להם אני מבטל דברי המקום ... אמרו לו: הרי סלע, כשם שאתה רוצה להוציא מסלע אחר, הוצא מזה. צווח עליהם "שמעו נא המורים"—המורים שיטין הרבה יש בו: המורים סרבנין, המורים שוטים, שכן בכרכי הים קורים לשוטים מורים. "וירם משה את ידו ויך את הסלע"—הכהו פעם אחת, התחיל הסלע נוטף מים מועטים... אמרו לו בן עמרם, הללו מים ליונקי שדים או לגמולי חלב? מיד הקפיד כנגדן והכהו פעמיים ויצאו מים רבים ושטפו כל מי שהיה מרנן כנגדן.

They began to say, "Moses knows how rocks work; if he wants, he can make water come out of this one." Moses found himself in a quandary: If I listen to them, I have disregarded the words of G-d… They said to him: "Here is a rock. The same way you intend to draw water out of that other rock, draw water out of this one here."

He yelled at them, "Listen, you *morim!*" There are multiple interpretations for this word. It can mean "obstinate ones." It can also mean "teachers," for in distant lands, the word "*morim*" means "teachers."

"Moses raised his hand and struck the rock." He struck it once, and a little water began to trickle out… They said to him, "Son of Amram, is this water for those who breastfeed or suckle on milk?" Moses immediately grew *indignant and struck it a second time, bringing forth much water which drowned whoever had rebelled.*

TEXT 9

Bamidbar 20:12

וַיֹּאמֶר ה' אֶל מֹשֶׁה וְאֶל אַהֲרֹן יַעַן לֹא הֶאֱמַנְתֶּם בִּי לְהַקְדִּישֵׁנִי לְעֵינֵי בְּנֵי יִשְׂרָאֵל לָכֵן לֹא תָבִיאוּ אֶת הַקָּהָל הַזֶּה אֶל הָאָרֶץ אֲשֶׁר נָתַתִּי לָהֶם:

G-d said to Moses and Aaron, "Since you did not have faith in Me to sanctify Me in the eyes of the children of Israel, therefore you shall not bring this assembly to the Land which I have given them. These are the Waters of Dispute [Mei Merivah] where the children of Israel contended with G-d, and He was sanctified through them.

Optional Section
Moses' Plea

TEXT 10A

Devarim (Deuteronomy) 3:23-25

וָאֶתְחַנַּן אֶל ה' בָּעֵת הַהִוא לֵאמֹר:

ה' אֱלוֹקִים אַתָּה הַחִלּוֹתָ לְהַרְאוֹת אֶת עַבְדְּךָ אֶת גָּדְלְךָ וְאֶת יָדְךָ הַחֲזָקָה אֲשֶׁר מִי אֵ-ל בַּשָּׁמַיִם וּבָאָרֶץ אֲשֶׁר יַעֲשֶׂה כְמַעֲשֶׂיךָ וְכִגְבוּרֹתֶךָ:

אֶעְבְּרָה נָּא וְאֶרְאֶה אֶת הָאָרֶץ הַטּוֹבָה אֲשֶׁר בְּעֵבֶר הַיַּרְדֵּן הָהָר הַטּוֹב הַזֶּה וְהַלְּבָנֹן:

I entreated G-d at that time, saying,

"O Lord G-d, You have begun to show Your ser-vant Your greatness and Your strong hand, for who is [like] G-d in heaven or on earth who can do as Your deeds and Your might?

Pray let me cross over and see the good land that is on the other side of the Jordan, this good mountain and the Lebanon."

TEXT 10B

Midrash Devarim Rabah 11:11

אמר משה לפני הקדוש ברוך הוא: רבונו של עולם אם אין אתה מכניס אותי לארץ ישראל, הניח אותי כחיות השדה שהן אוכלין עשבין ושותין מים וחיין ורואין את העולם, כך תהא נפשי כאחת מהן. אמר לו: רב לך. אמר לפניו רבונו של עולם, ואם לאו הניח אותי בעולם הזה כעוף הזה שהוא פורח בכל ד' רחות העולם ומלקט מזונו בכל יום, ולעת הערב חוזר לקינו, כך תהא נפשי כאחת מהן, אמר לו: רב לך.

Moses said to G-d, "Master of the Universe, if you do not allow me to enter the Land of Israel, at least let me live on as one of the animals of the field who eats grass and drinks water and lives and sees the world. My soul will be like one of theirs."

G-d said to him, "You have plenty."

Moses said to Him, "Master of the Universe, if not, then please let me stay in this world as a bird that flies in all four directions and gathers its food each day and each day it returns to its nest. My soul will be like one of theirs."

G-d said to Him, "You have plenty."

End Optional Section

Devarim Rabah

A homiletic commentary on the Book of Deuteronomy. It was first published in Constantinople in 1512, with four other Midrashic works on the other four books of the Pentateuch. The homilies are structured similarly; each episode begins with a question of religious law and is followed by an answer, which opens with the words, "Our sages taught." Most commentaries end with reassurances and promises of the redemption.

2. One Sin, 13 Explanations

TEXT 11

Rabbi Shmuel Dovid Luzzato, Shadal to Parashat Chukat

משה רבנו חטא חטא אחד, והמפרשים העמיסו עליו שלושה עשר חטאים ויותר ... אשר על כן נמנעתי מהעמק החקירה בדבר זה, מיראה שמא יצא לי פירוש חדש ונמצאתי גם אני מוסיף עוון חדש על משה רבנו.

Our teacher Moses committed one sin, and the commentaries saddle him with 13 sins or more… As such, I have abstained from delving into this matter, for fear that I would arrive at a new interpretation, and I too would attribute a new sin to Moses our teacher.

Cover-up for the Spies

TEXT 12

Rabbi Don Yitzchak Abarbanel, Bamibdar ch. 20

ודעתי בזה שמשה ואהרן שניהם נענשו בעבור עוונות שעשו. אם אהרן בעוון העגל ואם משה אדוננו ענין המרגלים. לא שהיה אהרן מעובדי העגל ולא שהיה משה מדור המרגלים, חלילה להם מרשע! אבל אהרן כמו שהתבאר במקומו שלא בכוונה רעה עשה את העגל... ואמנם חטא משה היה כי כאשר שאלו ישראל לשלוח מרגלים, לא שאלו אלא "וישיבו אותנו דבר את הדרך אשר נעלה בה"... ומשה אדוננו הוסיף מעצמו בשליחות... שיראו את העם היושב בארץ החזק הוא הרפה המעט הוא אם רב...

Moses and Aaron were punished for the sins they did. For Aaron, it was the sin of the Golden Calf, and for Moses our leader it was the matter of the spies. This is not to say that Aaron was amongst those who served the Golden Calf or that Moses was the same as the spies, Heaven forbid! Rather, Aaron—as explained in that context—constructed the calf with no negative intent...

Moses' fault was that when the Jews asked him to send spies, they only asked "Bring us back word by which route we shall go up..." Moses took the initiative to then add the task of seeing "If the people who inhabit the Land; are they strong or weak? Are there few or many?"

Rabbi Don Yitzchak Abarbanel
1437–1508
Biblical exegete and statesman. Abarbanel was born in Lisbon, Portugal and served as a minister in the court of King Alfonso V of Portugal. After intrigues at court led to accusations against him, he fled to Spain, where he once again served as a counselor to royalty. It is claimed that Abarbanel offered King Ferdinand and Queen Isabella large sums of money for the revocation of their Edict of Expulsion of 1492, but to no avail. After the expulsion, he eventually settled in Italy where he wrote a commentary on Scripture, as well as other venerated works.

TEXT 13A

Devarim (Deuteronomy) 1:26, 34-35, 37

וְלֹא אֲבִיתֶם לַעֲלֹת וַתַּמְרוּ אֶת פִּי ה' אֱלֹקֵיכֶם:...

וַיִּשְׁמַע ה' אֶת קוֹל דִּבְרֵיכֶם וַיִּקְצֹף וַיִּשָּׁבַע לֵאמֹר:

אִם יִרְאֶה אִישׁ בָּאֲנָשִׁים הָאֵלֶּה הַדּוֹר הָרָע הַזֶּה אֵת הָאָרֶץ הַטּוֹבָה אֲשֶׁר

נִשְׁבַּעְתִּי לָתֵת לַאֲבֹתֵיכֶם:...

גַּם בִּי הִתְאַנַּף ה' בִּגְלַלְכֶם לֵאמֹר גַּם אַתָּה לֹא תָבֹא שָׁם:

But you did not want to go up, and you re-belled against the commandment of the Lord, your G-d…

And G-d heard the sound of your words, and He be-came angry and swore, saying,

"If any of these men of this evil generation sees the good land, which I swore to give your forefathers…"

G-d was also angry with me because of you, saying, "Neither will you go there."

TEXT 13B

Abarbanel ad loc.

מה ראה משה רבינו עליו השלום להכניס גזרתו בתוך המרגלים בגזרתם
שלא יבואו אל הארץ?...

ואומר שדעתי בזה הוא... ומשה אדוננו מת בעון המרגלים... והיה אם
כן מי מריבה כלי אמצעי לדבר ולא סיבה עצמית בו.

Why did Moses mention the decree against him in the context of the decree against the spies that they would not come to the Land?

I think that this is because Moses died [and did not enter Israel] because of the sin of the spies... If so, the events at Mei Merivah *were just a proxy and were not the true reason.*

Anger

TEXT 14

Maimonides, Eight Chapters, Chapter 4

ואתה יודע שאדון הראשונים והאחרונים, משה רבנו, כבר אמר עליו
השם יתברך: "יען לא האמנתם בי להקדישני"... וחטאו עליו השלום
הוא, שנטה לצד אחד הקצוות במעלה אחת שבמעלות המידות, והיא
הסבלנות, כאשר נטה לצד הרגזנות באומרו: "שמעו נא המורים"...
דקדק עמו הקדוש ברוך הוא, שיהיה אדם כמוהו מתרגז לעיני עדת
ישראל במקום שאין הרגזנות ראויה, וכגון זה באדם שכמותו חילול

השם הוא, שכן תנועותיו כולן ודברותיו הכל למדים מהם... ואיך ייראו
בו הרגזנות והיא ממעשי הרעים כמו שביארנו...

וכאשר ראוהו שהתרגז, אמרו: ודאי אין הוא עליו השלום מאלה שיש
להם פחיתות מידה, ולולא ידע שהאלוקים התאנף בנו על דרישת
המים ושאנחנו הכעסנוהו יתברך, לא היה מתרגז. ואנו לא מצאנו לשם
יתברך שהתרגז או שכעס בדבריו עליו בעניין הזה, אלא אמר "קח את
המטה והקהל את העדה" וגו'...

הנה התרנו ספק מספקי התורה, שנאמרו בו דברים רבים ונשאל פעמים
רבות "איזה חטא חטא?"

Rabbi Moshe ben Maimon
(Maimonides, Rambam)
1135–1204

Halachist, philosopher, author, and physician. Maimonides was born in Cordoba, Spain. After the conquest of Cordoba by the Almohads, he fled Spain and eventually settled in Cairo, Egypt. There, he became the leader of the Jewish community and served as court physician to the vizier of Egypt. He is most noted for authoring the *Mishneh Torah*, an encyclopedic arrangement of Jewish law, and for his philosophical work, *Guide for the Perplexed*.

G-d said of the master of the early and latter ages, Moses our leader, "Since you did not have faith in Me to sanctify Me." Moses' sin was that he veered from that most important of character traits—patience. He veered to anger when he said, "Listen, you rebels!" G-d reasoned that when a man like Moses grows angry in front of the congregation of Israel in a place where anger is not justified, it causes a desecration of His name, because everyone learns from all his words and actions. How could they witness such anger in him, when it is one of the negative traits?

When they saw that he had become angry, they said, "He is certainly not prone to negative traits. If not for the fact that G-d Himself is angry that we demanded water and it is we who angered Him, Moshe would not be angry."

Yet, we do not find evidence of G-d being angry. He had simply said, "Take your staff and gather the people."

We have thus resolved one of the greatest conundrums of the Torah, about which much has been said, the question which has been asked repeatedly: What sin did Moshe do?

TEXT 15A

Nachmanides, Pirush Haramban Bamidbar 20:8

הוסיף הבל על הבלים שהכתוב אומר: "מריתם את פי", שעברו על דבריו ואמר "לא האמנתם בי" – שלא האמינו בו, ואין העונש בעבור שכעס ... ועוד כי אהרן לא כעס מימיו כי בשלום ובמישור הלך מעודו ...

He adds nonsense to nonsense, for the verse states, "You defied My word," meaning that they had gone against G-d's words. It states, "You did not have faith in Me," meaning that they did not have faith in G-d. The punishment was not because of anger... Furthermore, Aaron never grew angry in his life, for his way was one of peace and composure...

Rabbi Moshe ben Nachman
(Nachmanides, Ramban)
1194–1270

Scholar, philosopher, author and physician. Nachmanides was born in Spain and served as leader of Iberian Jewry. In 1263, he was summoned by King James of Aragon to a public disputation with Pablo Cristiani, a Jewish apostate. Though Nachmanides was the clear victor of the debate, he had to flee Spain because of the resulting persecution. He moved to Israel and helped reestablish communal life in Jerusalem. He authored a classic commentary on the Pentateuch and a commentary on the Talmud.

Suspect of Sorcery

TEXT 15B

Ibid.

והקרוב מן הדברים שנאמרו בזה והוא טוב לדחות השואל, הם דברי רבינו חננאל שכתב כי החטא הוא אומרם "המן הסלע הזה נוציא לכם מים" וראוי שיאמרו יוציא לכם ה' מים כדרך שאמרו "בתת ה' לכם בערב בשר לאכול"... ואולי חשבו העם כי משה ואהרן בחכמתם הוציאו להם מים מן הסלע, וזהו "לא קדשתם אותי [בתוך בני ישראל]".

The most plausible in all that was said in this regard, and which is a good rebuttal for questioners, are the words of Rabbeinu Chananel. He wrote that the sin was that they said, "Can *we* draw water for you from this rock?" They should have instead said, "Can G-d draw water," in the same way that they had said, "When G-d gives you in the evening meat to eat…" This left the possibility open for the people to think that Moses and Aaron, with their wisdom, would draw water from the rock. This is the meaning of [the verse:] "you did not sanctify Me [in the midst of the children of Israel]."

3. The Stuff a Jew is Made Of

Never Besmirch my Children!

TEXT 16

Midrash Pesiktah Derav Kahana §14

"ויצום אל בני ישראל" מה צום? אמר להם: אל תקרו לבני "מורים".
וכיון שהקניטו על מי מריבה, אמר להם משה: "שמעו נא המורים".
אמר להם הקדוש ברוך הוא: כל עצמי הייתי מצוה אתכם אל תקרו לבני
מורים, ואתם קורים לבניי מורים?! ... לכן ... לא תביאו.

The verse states "He commanded them [Moses and Aaron] concerning the children of Israel." What did He command them? He said to them, "Don't call My children 'rebels.'" When the Jews angered Moses at the Waters of Strife, he said to them, "Listen, you rebels!" G-d said to them: With all My being I commanded you not to call My children "rebels," and yet you call My children "rebels!?"... Therefore... "You shall not come [into the Land]."

TEXT 17

Rabbi Avraham ibn Ezra
1092–1167

Biblical commentator, linguist and poet. Ibn Ezra was born in Tuledo, Spain and fled the Almohad regime to other parts of Europe. It is believed that he was living in London at the time of his death. Ibn Ezra is best known for his literalistic commentary on the Pentateuch. He also wrote works of poetry, philosophy, medicine, astronomy, and other topics.

Rabbi Avraham Ibn Ezra, Bamibdar 20:8

יש בכאן פירושים רבים, יש בדברי יחיד, בעבור שאמר לישראל שמעו
נא המורים והם בני אברהם יצחק ויעקב.

There are many explanations about this issue, one individual [commentator] says: It was because he had told the Jewish people, "Listen, you rebels!"—and they are the children of Abraham, Isaac, and Jacob.

Elijah's Mistrust

TEXT 18

Pirkei Rabbi Eliezer

A Midrash bearing the name of Rabbi Eliezer ben Horkonus, a prominent rabbinic sage living during the 1st and 2nd centuries. *Pirkei Rabbi Eliezer* commences with the story of the early days Rabbi Eliezer's life and then chronologically narrates and expounds upon events from the Creation until the middle of the journeys of the Children of Israel in the wilderness.

Midrash Pirkei Derabbi Eliezer, ch. 28

נמלט ועמד אליהו זכרונו לברכה וברח לו להר חורב, שנאמר ויקם ויאכל
וישתה ושם נגלה לו הקדוש ברוך הוא. אמר לו: מה לך פה אליהו? קנא
קנאתי. אמר לו: לעולם אתה מקנא ... חייך שאין עושין ברית מילה עד
שאתה רואה בעיניך! מכאן התקינו חכמים לעשות כסא אחד מכובד
למלאך הברית שנקרא אליהו זכרונו לברכה מלאך הברית.

Elijah escaped to Mount Carmel, as it says, "And he arose and ate and drank, and he went." While he was there, G-d appeared to him. He said to him, "Elijah, why are you here?" [He answered] "I have been zealous [for the Lord, the G-d of Hosts, for the children of Israel have forsaken Your

covenant.]" G-d said to him, "You are forever zealous… I swear that no circumcision will be performed
until you see it with your eyes!" This is why the Sages
instructed that a special chair be set aside for the angel
of the brit, Elijah.

Postscript: How Could Moses Sin?

TEXT 19

Midrash Tanchuma, Vayeshev §4

זהו שאמר הכתוב "לכו [חזו] מפעלות אלקים נורא עלילה על בני אדם".
אמר רבי יהושע בן קרחה: אף הנוראות שאתה מביא עלינו, בעלילה
אתה מביאם ...

למה הדבר דומה? למי שמבקש לגרש את אשתו, כשביקש לילך לביתו
כתב גט, נכנס לביתו והגט בידו, [וכעת] מבקש עלילה ליתנו לה. אמר
לה: מזגי לי את הכוס שאשתה. מזגה לו, וכיון שנטל הכוס מידה, אמר
לה הרי זה גיטך. אמרה לו מה פשעי? אמר לה צאי מביתי שמזגת לי
כוס פשור. אמרה לו כבר היית יודע שאני עתידה למזוג לך כוס פשור?
ש[הרי] כתבת הגט והביאתו בידך!...

וכן הוא אומר "עתה תראה אשר אעשה לפרעה"—במלחמת פרעה
אתה רואה ואין אתה רואה במלחמת שלשים ואחד המלכים. וכיון
שאמר להם שמעו נא המורים, אמר לו הקב"ה לכן לא תביאו את הקהל
הזה. הוי נורא עלילה על בני אדם.

Tanchuma
A Midrashic work bearing
the name of Rabbi Tanchuma,
a 4th-century Talmudic
sage quoted often in
this work. This Midrash
provides textual exegeses
and stories, expounds upon
the biblical narrative, and
develops and illustrates
moral principles. *Tanchuma*
is unique in that many of its
sections commence with a
halachic discussion, which
subsequently leads into
non-halachic teachings.

The verse states, "Go and see the deeds of G-d, awesome in His pretexts toward mankind." Rabbi Yehoshua ben Korcha said: Even those awesome things You do for us, You do under a pretext.

What is this comparable to? A man who wishes to divorce his wife. He writes the get, walks into the house with it, and searches for a pretext to give it to her. He tells her, "Pour me something to drink." She pours it for him, and when he takes the cup for her, he says "Here is your get." She asks him, "What did I do wrong?" He tells her, "Leave my house, because you poured me a lukewarm cup." She responds, "Did you already know that I would pour you a lukewarm cup that you prepared the get and brought it in your hand?!"

In this vein the verse [where G-d addresses Moses early in his mission] states, "You shall see what I will do to Pharaoh"—you will see the war against Pharaoh, but you will not see the war of the 31 kings [in Israel]. And then when Moshe said, "Listen, you rebels!" G-d told him that he would not be able to bring this people into the Land. Thus, He is "awesome in His pretexts towards mankind."

Conclusion—The Rebbe

TEXT 20

The Lubavitcher Rebbe, Hayom Yom entry for 2 Elul

בני ישראל נקראו ארץ חפץ, שיש בהם כמה חפצים יקרים באהבת
השי"ת ויראתו ומדות טובות, ואין דבר גילוי המדות הטובות תלוי אלא
במעורר. דבר ברור הוא, אשר בכל חלקי האדמה נמצאים מעינות מים
חיים, וההבדל הוא רק בקירוב וריחוק, ואם כן הלא הכל תלוי בהחופר
וכח סבלנותו ומתינותו.

The Children of Israel are called "eretz cheif-etz," a desired land, for they possess numerous "precious articles" in the love and fear of G-d, and in fine character traits. Bringing these fine traits to the surface depends entirely upon the individual stimulating them. It is clear that throughout the earth are wellsprings of living water; the difference between them is only that some are near the surface, others far. Everything therefore depends on the well-digger, and the degree of his patience and perseverance.

Rabbi Menachem Mendel Schneerson
1902–1994
The towering Jewish leader of the 20th century, known as "the Lubavitcher Rebbe," or simply as "the Rebbe." Born in southern Ukraine, the Rebbe escaped Nazi occupied Europe, arriving in the U.S. in June 1941. The Rebbe inspired and guided the revival of traditional Judaism after the European devastation, impacting virtually every Jewish community the world over. The Rebbe often emphasized that the performance of just one additional good deed could usher in the era of Mashiach. The Rebbe's scholarly talks and writings have been printed in more than 200 volumes.

TEXT 21

The Lubavitcher Rebbe, Igrot Kodesh vol. 28 p. 157

אינו נכון כלל וכלל ובוודאי שאין זה רצון השם [לעזוב את השכונה].
וישאר כאן על כל פנים עד לאחר חודש תשרי הבא עלינו לטובה—
באופן שנוכל לחגוג ביחד את כל ג׳ הרגלים (וכן יום הולדתי)—כולל
שמחת תורה. וינצל הזמן ללימוד התורה ועיון בה בחיות ועד שיוכל
להחיות גם אחרים.

This is utterly incorrect, and [leaving the neighborhood] is certainly not what G-d wants. Stay here until at least after Tishrei, so that we will be able to celebrate the three Festivals [Pesach, Shavuot, Sukkot] (as well as my birthday)—including Simchat Torah, together. Use this time to learn Torah and delve into it with enthusiasm to the extent that you are able to enthuse others as well.

12

BALAK

The Joy of Joy

The Wisdom of Bilaam's Donkey

Student Manual

PARSHA OVERVIEW
Balak

Balak, the king of Moab, summons the prophet Balaam to curse the people of Israel. On the way, Balaam is berated by his donkey, who sees, before Balaam does, the angel that G-d sends to block their way. Three times, from three different vantage points, Balaam attempts to pronounce his curses; each time, blessings issue forth instead. Balaam also prophesies on the end of the days and the coming of Moshiach.

The people fall prey to the charms of the daughters of Moab, and are enticed to worship the idol Peor. When a high-ranking Israelite official publicly takes a Midianite princess into a tent, Pinchas kills them both, stopping the plague raging among the people.

1. The Amazing Animal

The Donkey Speaks

TEXT 1

Bamidbar 22:21-28

וַיָּקָם בִּלְעָם בַּבֹּקֶר וַיַּחֲבֹשׁ אֶת אֲתֹנוֹ וַיֵּלֶךְ עִם שָׂרֵי מוֹאָב:

וַיִּחַר אַף אֱלֹהִים כִּי הוֹלֵךְ הוּא וַיִּתְיַצֵּב מַלְאַךְ ה' בַּדֶּרֶךְ לְשָׂטָן לוֹ וְהוּא רֹכֵב עַל אֲתֹנוֹ וּשְׁנֵי נְעָרָיו עִמּוֹ:

וַתֵּרֶא הָאָתוֹן אֶת מַלְאַךְ ה' נִצָּב בַּדֶּרֶךְ וְחַרְבּוֹ שְׁלוּפָה בְּיָדוֹ וַתֵּט הָאָתוֹן מִן הַדֶּרֶךְ וַתֵּלֶךְ בַּשָּׂדֶה וַיַּךְ בִּלְעָם אֶת הָאָתוֹן לְהַטֹּתָהּ הַדָּרֶךְ:

וַיַּעֲמֹד מַלְאַךְ ה' בְּמִשְׁעוֹל הַכְּרָמִים גָּדֵר מִזֶּה וְגָדֵר מִזֶּה:

וַתֵּרֶא הָאָתוֹן אֶת מַלְאַךְ ה' וַתִּלָּחֵץ אֶל הַקִּיר וַתִּלְחַץ אֶת רֶגֶל בִּלְעָם אֶל הַקִּיר וַיֹּסֶף לְהַכֹּתָהּ:

וַיּוֹסֶף מַלְאַךְ ה' עֲבוֹר וַיַּעֲמֹד בְּמָקוֹם צָר אֲשֶׁר אֵין דֶּרֶךְ לִנְטוֹת יָמִין וּשְׂמֹאול:

וַתֵּרֶא הָאָתוֹן אֶת מַלְאַךְ ה' וַתִּרְבַּץ תַּחַת בִּלְעָם וַיִּחַר אַף בִּלְעָם וַיַּךְ אֶת הָאָתוֹן בַּמַּקֵּל:

וַיִּפְתַּח ה' אֶת פִּי הָאָתוֹן וַתֹּאמֶר לְבִלְעָם מֶה עָשִׂיתִי לְךָ כִּי הִכִּיתַנִי זֶה שָׁלֹשׁ רְגָלִים:

I n the morning Bilaam arose, saddled his she-donkey and went with the Moabite dignitaries.

G-d's wrath flared because he was going, and an angel of G-d stationed himself on the road to thwart him, and he was riding on his she-donkey, and his two servants were with him.

The she-donkey saw the angel of G-d stationed on the road with his sword drawn in his hand; so the she-donkey turned aside from the road and went into a field. Bilaam beat the she-donkey to get it back onto the road.

The angel of G-d stood in a path of the vineyards, with a fence on this side and a fence on that side.

The she-donkey saw the angel of G-d, and she was pressed against the wall. She pressed Bilaam's leg against the wall, and he beat her again.

The angel of G-d continued going ahead, and he stood in a narrow place, where there was no room to turn right or left.

The she-donkey saw the angel of G-d, and it crouched down under Bilaam. Bilaam's anger flared, and he beat the she-donkey with a stick.

G-d opened the mouth of the she-donkey, and she said to Bilaam, "What have I done to you that you have struck me these three times?"

Did the Donkey Really See?

TEXT 2A

Rabbi Moshe ben Nachman
(Nachmanides, Ramban)
1194–1270

Scholar, philosopher, author and physician. Nachmanides was born in Spain and served as leader of Iberian Jewry. In 1263, he was summoned by King James of Aragon to a public disputation with Pablo Cristiani, a Jewish apostate. Though Nachmanides was the clear victor of the debate, he had to flee Spain because of the resulting persecution. He moved to Israel and helped reestablish communal life in Jerusalem. He authored a classic commentary on the Pentateuch and a commentary on the Talmud.

Nachmanides, Pirush Haramban ad loc.

"ותרא האתון את מלאך ה'". מלאכי השם השכלים הנבדלים לא יראו לחוש העינים, כי אינם גוף נתפש במראה, וכאשר יראו לנביאים או לאנשי הרוח הקודש כדניאל ישיגו אותם במראות הנפש המשכלת כאשר תגיע למעלת הנבואה או למדרגה שתחתיה, אבל שיושגו לעיני הבהמה אי אפשר.

על כן תוכל לפרש "ותרא האתון", כי הרגישה בדבר מפחיד אותה מלעבור והוא המלאך אשר יצא לשטן...

ואמר "ותרא את מלאך ה' וחרבו שלופה בידו", לא שתראה חרב אף כי מלאך, אבל ירמוז הכתוב כי מפני היות המלאך נכון להכות בה חרדה חרדה גדולה נדמה לה כאלו באים לשחוט אותה.

"The she-donkey saw the angel of G-d." The angels are spiritual beings who cannot be perceived with physical eyes, for they do not have a body that can be perceived. When they do appear to prophets or to those imbued with Divine spirit (such as Daniel), they are perceived with "intellectual vision" when the individual reaches the state of prophecy. But it is impossible for the eyes of an animal to see these beings.

Thus, we can interpret the words, "And the she-donkey saw" to mean that she sensed a frightening force blocking her passage—which was the angel which had set out to thwart [Bilaam]…

When the Torah further states, "The she-donkey saw the angel of G-d... with his sword drawn in his hand," it does not mean that the donkey saw an angel or a sword, rather Scripture alludes to the fact that the angel instilled such a dread in the donkey that it appeared to her as if she was about to be slaughtered.

TEXT 2B

Rabbi Menachem ben Benyamin Recanati, Bamidbar ad loc.

ואנו לא נוכל להכחיש דברים הנוראים הנראים לעין תמיד.

We cannot deny these awesome words which are readily apparent to the beholder.

Rabbi Menachem ben Benyamin Recanati
ca. 1250–1310

Italian rabbi and kabbalist of note. He authored *Pirush Al Hatorah*, a mystical commentary on the Bible; *Pirush Hatefilot*, a commentary on the Sidur, and *Ta'amei Hamitzvot*, an explanation of the commandments. In addition, his halachic rulings are collected in his *Piskei Recanati*.

TEXT 3

Talmud Tractate Bava Kama 60b

תנו רבנן: כלבים בוכים, מלאך המות בא לעיר.

Our Rabbis taught: When dogs howl, [this is a sign that] the Angel of Death has come to town.

Babylonian Talmud

A literary work of monumental proportions that draws upon the legal, spiritual, intellectual, ethical, and historical traditions of Judaism. The 37 tractates of the Babylonian Talmud contain the teachings of the Jewish sages from the period after the destruction of the 2nd Temple through the 5th century CE. It has served as the primary vehicle for the transmission of the Oral Law and the education of Jews over the centuries; it is the entry point for all subsequent legal, ethical, and theological Jewish scholarship.

TEXT 4A

Rabbi Shlomo Yitschaki
(Rashi)
1040–1105

Most noted biblical and
Talmudic commentator.
Born in Troyes, France,
Rashi studied in the famed
yeshivot of Mainz and
Worms. His commentaries
on the Pentateuch and the
Talmud, which focus on the
straightforward meaning
of the text, have appeared
in virtually every edition
of the Talmud and Bible.

Rashi, Bamidbar ad loc.

"וַתֵּרֶא הָאָתוֹן". והוא לא ראה, שנתן הקדוש ברוך הוא רשות לבהמה לראות יותר מן האדם, שמתוך שיש בו דעת תטרף דעתו כשיראה מזיקין.

"The she-donkey saw." But Bilaam did not see, for G-d permitted a beast to perceive more than a man. Since he [man] possesses intelligence, he would become insane if he saw demons.

TEXT 4B

The Kehot Chumash, Bamidbar ad loc.

If G-d were to grant humans the perception to see angels, they would perforce see both benevolent and destructive angels (i.e., demons). Since the sight of destructive angels would be too overwhelming for most people, G-d generally does not grant humans this perception. But since animals do not have free choice and possess less sophisticated consciousness than humans, they are not frightened by the sight of destructive angels, so G-d allows them to see angels.

The Purpose of the Miracle

TEXT 5

Rabbi Bachaye ben Asher, Bamidbar ad loc.

על דרך הפשט דיבור האתון נס גדול וחוץ מדרך הטבע והיה זה לכבוד
ישראל, כי הקדוש ברוך הוא הפליא לעשות ורצה לשנות סדרי בראשית
בדיבור הבהמה לומר שאפילו הבהמה תכיר ותדע שאין השליחות הזה
ראוי להעשות... כי אפילו הבהמה שאין לה שכל תשכיל שאין ראוי
להסכים בקללת עם כי ברוך הוא.

O n the level of peshat, a talking donkey is a
great miracle that completely defies nature.
G-d performed this great miracle for the
honor of the Jewish people, to impart the message that
even an animal recognized that this was a mission not
worth undertaking... Even an animal that has limited
intellect appreciated that it is inappropriate to cooper-
ate in cursing a blessed nation.

Rabbi Bachaye ben Asher
ca. 1255–1340
Author of a work of Torah commentary, *Midrash Rabeinu Bachaye*; born in Saragossa, Spain. He is known for systemizing the four classic levels of exegesis: *peshat* (plain meaning), *remez* (allusive meaning), *derash* (homiletic exposition), and *sod* (kabbalistic meaning). He also authored a work on ethics, *Kad Hakemach*.

2. The Joy of Completeness

Three Times

TEXT 6

Rashi Bamidbar 22:28

"זה שלש רגלים". רמז לו אתה מבקש לעקור אומה החוגגת שלש
רגלים בשנה.

"These three times (regalim)." She hinted to him, "You seek to uproot a nation which celebrates three [primary] festivals (shalosh regalim) in a year?"

Reserved for the Spring

TEXT 7

Maimonides, Mishneh Torah, Laws of Festivals 6:17-18

שבעת ימי הפסח ושמונת ימי החג עם שאר ימים טובים כולם אסורים
בהספד ותענית, וחייב אדם להיות בהן שמח וטוב לב הוא ובניו ואשתו
ובני ביתו וכל הנלוים עליו שנאמר ושמחת בחגך וגו'... יש בכלל אותה
שמחה לשמוח הוא ובניו ובני ביתו כל אחד ואחד כראוי לו.

כיצד הקטנים נותן להם קליות ואגוזים ומגדנות, והנשים קונה להן
בגדים ותכשיטין נאים כפי ממונו, והאנשים אוכלין בשר ושותין יין
שאין שמחה אלא בבשר ואין שמחה אלא ביין.

I t is forbidden to fast or recite eulogies on the seven
days of Pesach, the eight days of Sukkot, and the
other holidays. On these days, a person is obligated
to be happy and in good spirits; he, his children, his
wife, the members of his household, and all those who
depend on him. As Scripture states, "And you shall
rejoice in your festivals."… Included in [this charge
to] rejoice is that he, his children, and the members
of his household should rejoice, each one in a manner
appropriate for him.

What is implied? Children should be given roasted
seeds, nuts, and sweets. For women, one should buy
nice clothes and jewelry according to one's financial ca-
pacity. Men should eat meat and drink wine, for there
is no happiness without partaking of meat nor wine.

**Rabbi Moshe
ben Maimon**
(Maimonides, Rambam)
1135–1204
Halachist, philosopher, author,
and physician. Maimonides
was born in Cordoba, Spain.
After the conquest of Cordoba
by the Almohads, he fled
Spain and eventually settled
in Cairo, Egypt. There, he
became the leader of the
Jewish community and served
as court physician to the vizier
of Egypt. He is most noted
for authoring the *Mishneh
Torah*, an encyclopedic
arrangement of Jewish law,
and for his philosophical work,
Guide for the Perplexed.

An Eternal Nation

TEXT 8

Rabbi Yehudah Loewe of Prague, Gur Aryeh to Rashi ad loc.

החורף אינו בכלל הזמן, כי הוא העדר והפסד הצמחים. ולפיכך אמר "וכי
אתה רוצה לאבד אומה שלימה החוגגת ג' פעמים בשנה", המורה על

נצחיות האומה, שיש להם זמני שמחה בראשית הזמן, אמצעו, וסופו. כי הרגלים הם זמן שמחה, והשמחה מורה על שלימות ועל המציאות, והאבל הוא על היפך, דהוא הפסד דבר, ולכך מתאבלין על מיתת המת. וישראל מציאותם בכל הזמנים; בראשיתו ובאמצעיתו וסופו, לכך יש להם לשמוח בשלש רגלים שהם בקיץ, שהוא המשך זמן המציאות. ולא נתן אותם בחורף, שהוא הפסד, ואינו מציאות. והדבר שיש לו דבר נצחי - איך באת לאבד.

Rabbi Yehudah Loew
(Maharal of Prague)
1525–1609

Talmudist and philosopher. Maharal rose to prominence as leader of the famed Jewish community of Prague. He is the author of more than a dozen works of original philosophic thought, including *Tiferet Yisrael* and *Netsach Yisrael*. He also authored *Gur Aryeh*, a supercommentary to Rashi's biblical commentary, and a commentary on the non-legal passages of the Talmud. He is buried in the Old Jewish Cemetery of Prague.

Winter is not considered part of "time," for it is a period of loss and death of vegetation. This, then, is what Rashi states, "You seek to uproot a nation which celebrates three festivals in a year?" The fact that the Jews celebrate these three festivals demonstrates their lasting power, for they celebrate at the beginning, middle, and end of time. The festivals are a time of joy, and joy demonstrates completion and assertiveness, whereas mourning is the opposite—a feeling of loss; hence we mourn the dead.

The Jews endure throughout the entire gamut of time—in the beginning, middle, and end. Thus, they celebrate three festivals in the spring and summer months which is the real "time," and not in the winter, which is a period of erosion and therefore insignificant.

[Accordingly, the donkey told Bilaam,] "How can you expect to destroy something with such lasting power?!"

3. Spiritual Battle

Rav Ashi and King Menasheh

TEXT 9

Talmud Tractate Sanhedrin 102b

רב אשי אוקי אשלשה מלכים. אמר: למחר נפתח בחברין.

אתא מנשה איתחזי ליה בחלמיה. אמר: חברך וחבירי דאבוך קרית
לן? מהיכא בעית למישרא המוציא? אמר ליה: לא ידענא. אמר ליה:
מהיכא דבעית למישרא המוציא לא גמירת, וחברך קרית לן? אמר ליה:
אגמריה לי, ולמחר דרישנא ליה משמך בפירקא. אמר ליה: מהיכא
דקרים בישולא.

אמר ליה: מאחר דחכימתו כולי האי, מאי טעמא קא פלחיתו
לעבודה זרה?

אמר ליה: אי הות התם - הות נקיטנא בשיפולי גלימא ורהטת אבתראי.

In the college of Rabbi Ashi, the lecture [one day]
terminated at "Three Kings." "Tomorrow," he said,
"we will commence with our colleagues."

*[That night] Menasheh came and appeared to him
in a dream. "You have called us your colleagues and
the colleagues of your father [let us see if you truly
are a comparable scholar]: From what part [of the
bread] is [the piece for reciting] the hamotzi blessing
to be taken?"*

"I do not know," he answered.

"You have not learned this," he jibed, "yet you call us your colleagues?!"

"Teach it to me," Rabbi Ashi begged, "and tomorrow I will teach it in your name at the session."

He answered, "From the part that is baked into a crust."

He then questioned him, "If you are so wise, why did you worship idols?"

He replied, "Were you there, you would have lifted up the hem of your garment and sped after me [to join me]!"

TEXT 10

Rabbi Yehudah Loewe of Prague, Netzach Yisrael ch. 3

רב אשי היה סובר כי היו טועים אחר העבודה זרה, ולא היה הדבר הזה משום יצרם הרע שהיה גובר בם, רק בשביל שלא היו חכמים כל כך, ולכך טעו אחר העבודה זרה.

והשיב לו, כי דבר זה אינו, כי חכמים היו, רק בשביל שהיה היצר גובר בם היו עובדים עבודה זרה. ואילו היה הוא באותו דור היה רץ אחריה, והוי נקיט בשיפולא גלימא. כי כאשר החוטא הוא חכם, ויודע שהוא חוטא, רק שהוא אינו יכול למשול על יצרו, הוא חפץ ואוהב שיבוא לו מונע עד שלא יוכל לחטוא. אבל הסכל, אדרבא, אם יבא לו מניעה - מסיר הוא המניעה, כי אינו יודע כמה גדול חטאו.

לכך אמר אילו הוית התם, לא היית עושה כמו שעושה החכם שהוא חפץ שיבוא לו מניעה אל החטא, אבל אתה אם היה בא לך מניעה, כמו

262 *Torah Studies* Season Three 5775

הגלימא שהיה מעכב עליך שלא לרוץ אחר העבודה זרה, נקיטת אותו
בשניך כדי שלא יעכב עליך לרוץ אחר עבודה זרה, כי אין אתה חכם
כל כך כמו באותו דור. שהם בודאי היו חפצים שיבוא להם מעכב שלא
יחטאו, כי ידעו כמה גדול החטא.

Rabbi Ashi figured that the three kings chased after idols simply because they were fools, as opposed to doing so because of feeling overwhelmed by the Evil Inclination.

Menasheh replied that this was not the case; they were actually great scholars, and it was their Evil Inclinations which overwhelmed them and drove them to idolatry.

Menasheh continued, "Were you there, you would have lifted up the hem of your garment and sped after me!" When a scholar sins and acknowledges his sin and recognizes that he is at the mercy of his urges, he hopes that some external force will prevent him from sinning. But when a thoughtless person sins, the opposite is true: if something stands in the way of his urges, he removes the obstacle and continues, for he doesn't recognize the gravity of his sins.

This, then, is what Menasheh meant, "If you were there, you wouldn't have acted as an intelligent person who hopes for the obstacle, rather you would have removed the obstacle—for example, the cloak that would hinder your pursuit of idolatry; you would hold it between your teeth so it shouldn't stop you from *running, for you are not as wise as the people of my generation!" Menasheh and his ilk certainly wished for obstacles to come their way, for they knew the gravity of their sins.*

In Divine Service

TEXT 11A

Rabbi Shmuel Bornstein
1855–1926

Chasidic rebbe of Sochaczev and author of the *Shem MiShmuel*, a chasidic commentary on the Torah.

Rabbi Shmuel Bornsztain, Shem Mishmuel, Parashat Balak 5670

בעבדות השם יתברך, יש שני מיני עבדות, אחת שעושה מחמת הציווי שנצטוה על זה, ואינו יכול לפטור את עצמו מזה, ואילו היתה לו מניעה ומקום לפטור את עצמו מזה היה פוטר את עצמו כי באמת כבד עליו הדבר. ויש שעושה רצון השם יתברך מחמת שבאמת הוא רצונו לעשות כרצונו יתברך, ואף אם היתה לו מניעה היה מסלק את המניעה בכל כחו כדי לעשות רצון השם יתברך, מאחר כי עצם רצונו הוא לעשות רצונו יתברך לא לפטור את עצמו מחמת החיוב שעליו.

וההיכר שבין שני מיני העובדים הנ"ל יבחן אם העבודה שעושה היא בשמחה ומתגעגע אחריה ומצפה לה לומר מתי תבוא לידי ואקיימנה, כדרך שאמר רבי עקיבא נשמתו עדן, זה סימן שהוא מהכת העובדים השם יתברך בשלימות, ואם אינו עושה בשמחה הוא סימן שאינו עושה רק מצד ההכרח להשלים חקו ולשלם החוב שעליו.

There are two ways to serve G-d: Some serve G-d because they are commanded to do so and cannot get themselves out of it; if there is any way to get out of it, they would grab the opportunity for they see it as a burden. Some, however, serve G-d because they truly wish to do so; if there is anything in the way, they seek to remove the obstacle with whatever means possible to do the will of G-d, because they really wish to fulfill G-d's will and not get out of it.

A sure way to determine the difference between these two approaches is to see if the person serves G-d with joy. If the person eagerly awaits the opportunity to serve G-d (as did Rabbi Akiva when he said, "When will I have the opportunity to give my life for G-d?" when he was martyred)—this indicates that he is among those who serve G-d wholeheartedly. But if he does not do it with joy, the indication is that he is acting as if under duress, strictly to discharge his obligation.

Having Your Cake and Eating it too

TEXT 11B

Ibid.

וישראל... כל מה שעושין עבודת ה' בשמחה עושין, וכמו עליית הרגלים אף שבאמת מצוה קשה מאד שלש פעמים בשנה לעזוב הפקר כל ביתם ולעלות לירושלים, מכל מקום הם עושין זאת בתכלית השמחה. וזהו שאמר אומה החוגגת שלש רגלים, דחגיגה היא לשון שמחה.

The Jews serve G-d with joy. Like the festivals: It is truly very difficult to fulfill a mitzvah that requires one to abandon their homes three times a year and make a pilgrimage to Jerusalem, yet the Jews do it with extreme joy.

This, then, is what the donkey said, "…a nation that celebrates three festivals." The focus here is the fact that they are joyous about it.

Bilaam Realizes

TEXT 12A

Bamidbar 23:24

הֶן עָם כְּלָבִיא יָקוּם וְכַאֲרִי יִתְנַשָּׂא לֹא יִשְׁכַּב עַד יֹאכַל טֶרֶף וְדַם חֲלָלִים יִשְׁתֶּה:

Behold, a people that rises like a lioness and raises itself like a lion. It does not lie down until it eats its prey and drinks the blood of the slain.

TEXT 12B

Rashi ad loc.

"הן עם כלביא יקום וגו'". כשהן עומדים משנתם שחרית, הן מתגברין כלביא וכארי לחטוף את המצות, ללבוש טלית לקרוא את שמע ולהניח תפילין.

Behold, a people that rises like a lioness: *When they awaken from their sleep in the morning they show the vigor of a lioness and a lion in grasping* mitzvot—*to don a* tallit, *recite the Shema and put on* tefillin.

Conclusion

TEXT 13

Rabbi Dovber Shneuri, Igrot Kodesh Admur Ha'emtzai, p. 265

צריך להיות שמחה של מצוה כפשוטה שבהנחת תפילין וטלית או
מעשה הצדקה ישמח מאד בהרגשת לב בשר דוקא על אשר עשה
נחת רוח ליוצרו. ואם גם לוקח לעצמו תענוג ושמחה זהו דוקא עיקר
ענין שמחה של מצוה.

One must literally experience joy when fulfilling a mitzvah. When [for example] putting on tefillin, donning a tallit, or giving charity, one's heart should fill with a palpable sense of joy over the fact that he gave pleasure to his Creator. The ultimate expression of joy of mitzvot is when one feels a personal sense of joy and pleasure.

Rabbi Dovber of Lubavitch
(Mitteler Rebbe)
1773–1827
Rabbi Dovber was the eldest son of and successor to Rabbi Shneur Zalman of Liadi and greatly expanded upon and developed his father's groundbreaking teachings. He was the first Chabad rebbe to live in the village of Lubavitch. Dedicated to the welfare of Russian Jewry, at that time confined to the Pale of Settlement, he established Jewish agricultural colonies. His most notable works on Chasidic thought include *Sha'ar Hayichud*, *Torat Chayim*, and *Imrei Binah*.

THE ROHR
Jewish Learning Institute

822 Eastern Parkway, Brooklyn, New York 11213

CHAIRMAN
Rabbi Moshe Kotlarsky
Lubavitch World Headquarters,
New York

PRINCIPAL
BENEFACTOR
Mr. George Rohr
New York, NY

EXECUTIVE DIRECTOR
Rabbi Efraim Mintz

ADMINISTRATOR
Dubi Rabinowitz

DIRECTOR OF
OPERATIONS
Rabbi Levi Kaplan

EXECUTIVE
COMMITTEE
Rabbi Chaim Block
San Antonio, TX

Rabbi Hesh Epstein
Columbia, SC

Rabbi Ronnie Fine
Montreal, Quebec

Rabbi Yosef Gansburg
Toronto, Ontario

Rabbi Shmuel Kaplan
Potomac, MD

Rabbi Yisrael Rice
S. Rafael, CA

Rabbi Avrohom Sternberg
New London, CT

TORAH STUDIES

CHAIRMAN
Rabbi Yosef Gansburg
Toronto, Ontario

DIRECTOR
Rabbi Meir Hecht
Chicago, IL

ADMINISTRATOR
Zalman Margolin
Brooklyn, NY

MANAGING EDITOR
Rabbi Ahrele Loschak
Brooklyn, NY

STEERING COMMITTEE
Rabbi Levi Fogelman
Natick, MA

Rabbi Yaakov Halperin
Allentown, PA

Rabbi Nechemiah Schusterman
Peabody, MA

Rabbi Ari Sollish
Atlanta, GA

CONTENT EDITORS
Rabbi Sholom Ber Notik
Brooklyn, NY

Shmuel Loebenstein
Brooklyn, NY

MARKETING AND PR
Rabbi Zalman M. Abraham
Sheva Rivkin

JLI CENTRAL
Brooklyn, NY

TEXTBOOK DESIGN
Mrs. Nechama Dina Hecht
Greenfield, MA

Mendel Schtroks
Brooklyn, NY

COPYEDITING
Mr. Michael Barnett
Bel Air, MD

POWERPOINT DESIGN
Rabbi Cheski Edelman
Olympia, WA

PRODUCTION
Rabbi Mendel Sirota
Brooklyn, NY

An affiliate of
Merkos L'Inyonei Chinuch
The Educational Arm of the Worldwide
Chabad Lubavitch Movement

Aug 9th new Temple

JEWISH LEARNING INSTITUTE

THE JEWISH LEARNING MULTIPLEX

Brought to you by the Rohr Jewish Learning Institute

In fulfillment of the mandate of the Lubavitcher Rebbe, of blessed memory,
whose leadership guides every step of our work,
the mission of the Rohr Jewish Learning Institute is to transform
Jewish life and the greater community through the study of Torah,
connecting each Jew to our shared heritage of Jewish learning.

While our flagship program remains the cornerstone of our organization,
JLI is proud to feature additional divisions catering to specific populations,
in order to meet a wide array of educational needs.

THE ROHR JEWISH LEARNING INSTITUTE,
a subsidiary of *Merkos L'Inyonei Chinuch*,
is the adult education arm of the Chabad-Lubavitch Movement.

TORAH STUDIES

Torah Studies provides a rich and nuanced encounter with the weekly Torah reading.

MYSHIUR
TALMUD LEARNING INITIATIVE

MyShiur courses are designed to assist students in developing the skills needed to study Talmud independently.

SINAI SCHOLARS SOCIETY
IN PARTNERSHIP WITH CHABAD ON CAMPUS

This rigorous fellowship program invites select college students to explore the fundamentals of Judaism.

JLI TEENS
YOUNG SMART JEWISH
IN PARTNERSHIP WITH CTEEN: CHABAD TEEN NETWORK

Jewish teens forge their identity as they engage in Torah study, social interaction, and serious fun.

ROSHCHODESH society

The Rosh Chodesh Society gathers Jewish women together once a month for intensive textual study.

TORAHCafé

TorahCafe.com provides an exclusive selection of top-rated Jewish educational videos.

National JEWISH RETREAT
BRILLIANT LEARNING, NATURALLY

This yearly event rejuvenates mind, body, and spirit with a powerful synthesis of Jewish learning and community.

The LAND & the SPIRIT
ISRAEL EXPERIENCE

Mission participants delve into our nation's rich past while exploring the Holy Land's relevance and meaning today.

JLI ACADEMY
PEDAGOGY · CURRICULUM · MARKETING

Select affiliates are invited to partner with peers and noted professionals, as leaders of innovation and excellence.

מכון שמואל

THE SAMI ROHR RESEARCH INSTITUTE

Machon Shmuel is an institute providing Torah research in the service of educators worldwide.

Newport
between Atlantic & Ventnor
Paid parking - four quarters

CMSW
Sharon Carrocia - Galloway -°

652-6040

re: Donna Golden